OFFALY HU

with Brian Lowry

www.**HERO**BOOKS.digital

HEROBOOKS

PUBLISHED BY HERO BOOKS
1 WOODVILLE GREEN
LUCAN
CO. DUBLIN
IRELAND

Hero Books is an imprint of Umbrella Publishing Ltd.
First Published 2022

A CIP record for this book is available from the British Library

ISBN 9781910827437

Cover design and formatting: jessica@viitaladesign.com
Ebook formatting: www.ebooklaunch.com
Photographs: Sportsfile

★ DEDICATION ★

To my three kids
Finn, Shay and Emilia Jane

And all the players who have worn the green, white
and gold down through the years

★ CONTENTS ★

★ ACKNOWLEDGEMENTS ★

BEING AN OFFALY supporter in the 90s was something special.

It was a magical time to be a young teenager and following Offaly. The hurlers one week and the footballers the next… Croke Park was Offaly's home as the Leinster Championship swung into action each year.

The normal mode of transport from the sticks to the big smoke was my father's Toyota HiAce van. A builder's van during the week, it had three seats in the front but it was the back of the van where the magic happened.

More often than not, the homemade bench similar to those in a church would be loaded up on the Sunday morning. Myself and anyone else that didn't make the cut for the front three seats would pile in.

The 1994 All-Ireland hurling final was the *day* of days.

I was in the upper deck of the Hogan Stand with my father. With 10 minutes to go, things weren't looking good and Limerick folk were already celebrating.

Offaly supporters were starting to drift away to beat the traffic.

Inside, I was wondering would we be the next to leave.

But there was no fear.

After Offaly blitzed Limerick to claim the All-Ireland, the final whistle had barely sounded and I was been navigated through the hysterical crowd by my father... and bolstered up over the fencing and out onto the pitch.

It was devotion back then.

Offaly supporters planned their weeks and months around fixtures, and the players that pulled on the green, white and gold gave us some days.

During all the success, my father was chairman of our club, Ferbane GAA. The scramble for tickets was eye-opening at the time and being so close to the build-up to the big days was amazing.

Homecomings and school visits after Leinster and All-Ireland titles were almost annual.

I was immersed in it all.

TO MY PARENTS Jimmy and Alice, there is no way I would be in such a privileged position writing this book without the GAA bug that you instilled in me.

I will be forever grateful for the opportunities and experiences that you have given me, not just through the GAA, but in life in general

We wouldn't be ones for telling each other how we feel, but I hope you know the impact you have had on my life.

To my wife Claire, your support and understanding may seem like a small thing but it was integral to this project. You have been a great sounding-board and the constant voice of reason, while all the time, keeping the show on the road. Behind every man is an even better woman and our three kids and I are lucky to have you as a wife and mother.

To Liam Hayes and the team at Hero Books, thank you for putting your trust in me and giving me the great privilege of putting this book together. Your patience was tested on more than one occasion, so thanks for sticking by me.

I am surrounded by many great colleagues in my line of work. In particular the help and advice of Michael Verney has been immense and for that I am very grateful.

There are a lot of cogs in the wheel, but when it comes down to it, the 25 players who gave their time and memories to me are the ones that made this happen. Thank you for your time, hospitality and humour along the way.

Many of you were heroes of mine growing up, and to have the opportunity to sit down and shoot the breeze is something that will always make me very grateful.

Life comes and goes, but memories last forever. And I hope this book has done justice to the fantastic memories you have given Offaly supporters over the years.

Uíbh Fhailí Abú!
Brian Lowry
February 2022

JOHNNY FLAHERTY

KILKENNY 3-9 OFFALY 0-16
Leinster SHC Final
Croke Park
JULY 20, 1969

Johnny Flaherty beats Sylvie Linnane and Seamus Coen of Galway in the 1981 All-Ireland final, 12 years after the 'Game of his Life' in a first Leinster final with Offaly.

★ **OFFALY:** D Martin; P Spellman, D Flanagan, J Murphy; B Moylan, J Kirwan (0-1), E Fox; JJ Healion (0-2), D Hanniffy (0-1); G 'Speedy' Burke (0-1), PJ Whelahan, **J Flaherty (0-3)**; P Mulhare (0-1), W Gorman, P Molloy (0-7). Subs: M Kirwan for Flanagan, P Moylan for Fox, T Dooley for Burke.

★ **KILKENNY:** O Walsh; T Carroll, P Dillon, J Treacy: W Murphy, P Henderson, M Coogan; P Moran, M Lalor; P Lalor, P Delaney (3-0), E Keher (0-5); J Miller (0-1), J Lynch (0-1), M Brennan (0-2). Subs: G Cooke for P Lalor, S Buckley for Lynch.

THE ACTION

IT WAS A case of so close, but yet so far, as the Offaly hurlers ruffled Kilkenny feathers in the 1969 Leinster final, before coming out on the wrong side of a two-point defeat after a classic encounter in Croke Park.

Having already taken out Wexford in the semi-final, Offaly proved they were no flash in the pan and had Kilkenny rattled for long periods. In the end, three Pat Delaney goals proved crucial as the wait for a breakthrough in Leinster continued.

The goals were crucial and Delaney's strikes just before half-time to level the game, and his third late into the second-half, were killer blows for an Offaly team, who had the class in the forward line to hit 16 points, where Paddy Molloy and the crafty Johnny Flaherty led the way.

Offaly roared out of the traps and went 0-3 to 0-0 up inside the opening five minutes with Molloy, JJ Healion and Flaherty all opening their accounts. Kilkenny settled down, however, and the first of Delaney's goals helped them take the lead just over midway through the half.

Undaunted, Offaly came again and the deadly free-taking of Molloy, coupled with another beauty from Flaherty, had them leading by three points coming up to half-time, before Delaney struck with his second sucker-punch to leave them all square, 0-10 to 2-4.

Offaly were on top in the second-half with Molloy to the fore, but just as it looked like they would pull off something special, Kilkenny struck for goal number three after Delaney pounced on the rebound, after Damien Martin had made a fantastic save.

Offaly wilted somewhat at this juncture as Kilkenny pulled three ahead. The Faithful County got a point back, but it wasn't enough as they fell in the end by two points.

★★★★★

"

I WAS AWFUL disappointed in 1969, to tell you the truth. We had a great chance of winning that Leinster final. I thought we showed too much loyalty to some of the older players. We had reached an under-21 final in 1967 and we were only beaten by a point by Dublin.

There were some magnificent hurlers on that panel, but they were never brought on. Those lads went on to prove that afterwards.

We were too loyal, and some players just held their positions because that's the way it was in Offaly back then. It has to be said that they were great men and had served Offaly well, but it was a great pity because we would have turned the tide that day if we had been a bit more ambitious.

We had the makings of a very good team, but we had no view for the future. It was all just day-by-day. There were a few positions that we needed to fill and that takes a few years; it doesn't happen overnight.

We had them rattled. You couldn't expect the older lads to keep up the pressure, to be fair to them. That was a very good Kilkenny team. Eddie Keher was at his best at that time. Pat Henderson, Martin Coogan... they were all magnificent.

I just think the breakthrough that eventually came in the early 80s should have come in 1969. We made no in-roads until the late 70s after that.

We had played the All-Ireland champions Wexford in the semi-final and we beat them. Offaly won three great games that day, as the senior and minor footballers also prevailed.

The final against Kilkenny was about putting up a good show, that was the height of the ambition. We were missing a great player that day in Brendan Barry. He went to England and he wasn't brought home, for whatever reason... I don't know.

He was a three-point man every day. Little things like that make a huge difference.

We still shouldn't have been beaten. I was in super form the same day. They put me into the right corner-forward position... the only time I played there before was in the semi-final win over Wexford.

Then I was brought out on Martin Coogan, who in my eyes was one of the greatest wing backs of all times. The distance he took me from goals – I was hurling the Kilkenny puck-out. By the time I got the ball, I was pucking it back to where I should have been myself.

I got three points alright, but I was too far from goals. I felt with the form I was in – and even though I played very well – we would have been depending on Paddy Molloy and myself for the majority of our scores.

We got 16 points, which was a good return. We were one of the highest scoring teams in the country at the time when it came to points' totals.

Damien Martin only came into the goals for the championship in 1969. He was the best goalkeeper in Offaly for years before that but, for whatever reason, he wasn't brought in until 1969. He was an All Star goalkeeper in 1971... and he *only* the number one goalkeeper since '69.

Quite a few of the players had the belief, but there were probably others who didn't and had the feeling that it was a day out.

Younger players had come on by the late 70s and early 80s. They were very skilful, disciplined and dependable. Those things maybe weren't there in the 60s. It made that three and four points of a difference.

Everyone was saying that if we put up a good show, people would be happy. That was the attitude at the time. I wasn't too happy about that, and it spurred me on a good bit more, to be honest.

I wasn't overawed by Kilkenny. I found it a lot easier to hurl against the top counties than club, or anything like that. The higher they took the game, the better I seemed to hurl.

Wexford had beaten Tipperary in the All-Ireland final in 1968, and Kilkenny in the Leinster final in that same year. They had big names at that time – Willie Murphy, the Quigleys, Mick Jacob... and Tony Doran who was only early in his career. They were down 10 points against Tipperary in that 1968 final and they came back to win it.

I got a dose of hives before that semi-final with Wexford... on the Thursday, Friday and the Saturday. I had no hope of playing the game, but I went.

They gave me this and that... told me I was great and that I would be alright. It was like the magic water nowadays. I went out anyway and went in corner-forward. I was marking Ned Colfer and I got two goals and a couple of points off him. Paddy Molloy did the same the other side, so we were flying.

All this was without Barney Moylan, who was in Canada at the time. Pat Joe Whelahan, Speedy Burke and JJ Healion were there; we got the momentum and the further the game went on, the better we got.

Maybe Wexford underestimated us, I don't know. We hurled really well and it set us up nicely for the final. You could see we were good enough, fit enough, anxious enough, and determined enough, but we needed fresh faces that weren't there until the start of the 70s.

There was a big change then all of a sudden, when five or six lads left the panel and it took a few years to see who would step up to it. I went to America in 1971... that didn't help too much either.

I was brought home from America in 1973 and '74. We played Kilkenny in one of them and Wexford in the other. I needed to be there! I was the experienced forward at the time, with Paddy Molloy gone.

I came on the scene in 1966 and its funny, actually, the first game I played... they never even told me that I was on the team. I had heard it on the Saturday night that I was on the team, but no one from the management had said anything to me.

I brought my gear anyway. I was going into the game in Birr the next day and Willie Gorman met me and asked me where my gear was? So I knew then it must be true and it wasn't someone setting me up.

I went back out to car and got my gear.

We played Dublin in the league and drew with them. Waterford came to play us two weeks later, and we beat them. The next game in 1966 was Tipperary, and we beat them in Birr. It was an All-Ireland in itself.

It really set us up for 1967, but then the 'Battle of Birr' in 1967 washed us out completely that year.

We got back into it in 1968 and we played Kilkenny in Portlaoise. We had a man sent off early and Kilkenny only beat us by two points. So, the signs were there from a few years before 1969.

Myself and Brendan Barry both started off in 1966 and we made a big difference. It was roughly six points a game between the two of us. Throw in Paddy Molloy and Barney Moylan, and you had a fair forward line going through.

We were unlucky in 1967. The attitude got into the team that we could do what we liked. We played Westmeath in Birr and that shouldn't have been much of a problem. But we didn't want to beat them on the scoreboard... we wanted to beat them every which way. Three of us got sent off, including myself.

It was a pure disaster.

In 1967 we got to the under-21 final and we had a lovely team. Dublin beat us by one point. We should have won it.

I had the most important ball of the game. I did everything right. I drew everyone to the left-hand side of the goal and threw it over to my right-hand side, and hit a brilliant shot. The Dublin keeper fired the hurl across the goals and, would you believe, it hit the middle of the hurl and it spun up over the bar.

I couldn't believe it. I can laugh about it now, but I will never forget it. He threw the hurl and, to be honest, I'm not even sure if throwing a hurl like that was a foul back then.

We all had cars and, in fairness, John Dowling was a great administrator. We got fed after training and things were done well. There were no complaints there.

We would get fed in Egan's Hotel after training. Cards games were brought in to get lads together and have a bit of fun. It was definitely the start of something.

At that time, for every pound that was spent on the footballers, there was 50 pence spent on the hurlers – and it should have been the other way around as hurling would cost a lot more.

St Rynagh's and Kinnitty were the coming clubs at the time. That brought new thinking and new ideas. We were able to pass the ball to one another and talk to one another. That was the start of it.

We were doing well and the influx of new players from the likes St Rynagh's and Kinnitty really helped to change the thinking, and remove the animosity that was there for years. There was even a thing where players from rival clubs wouldn't pass the ball to each other. It was shocking, but slowly, surely, lads were able to go out and hurl hard against one another one week and come together for the county the following week.

Offaly were never going to win an All-Ireland until we sorted the likes of that out.

MICK SPAIN

BIRR 2-10 ST RYNAGH'S 2-9
Offaly SHC Final
St Brendan's Park, Birr
NOVEMBER 27, 1971

Mick Spain is honoured by GAA president John Horan (right) and Denis O'Callaghan of AIB at the GAA President's Awards in Croke Park in 2019.

★ **BIRR:** M Hennessy; G O'Meara, **M Spain**, H Hennessy; J Hernon (0-3), J Cleary, B Colahan; Bro Acquin, M Gleeson; D Hennessy (1-3), M Loughnane (0-1), S Hanniffy; P Goonan (0-1), T O'Shea (0-1), M Sammon. Subs: E Nevin (1-1) for Sammon, J Rafter for Hanniffy, D Kirwan for Goonan.

★ **ST RYNAGH'S:** D Martin; N Gallagher, F Whelahan, A Horan; S Moylan, P Moylan, H Dolan; R Johnson, PJ Whelahan; P Mulhare (1-1), B Moylan (1-8), B Lyons; M Moylan, P Horan, G Burke. Subs: M Hough for Lyons, J Horan for M Moylan.

THE ACTION

BIRR WOULD GO on to become one of the greatest forces in club hurling in more recent times, but it wasn't always the case. In 1971 they claimed the Offaly senior hurling title for the first time in 23 years, edging out their nearest and dearest rivals, St Rynagh's by a point.

A thrilling final was played in front of what was described in one newspaper report as, *One of the biggest crowds seen at a hurling final for years.* Birr were the rank outsiders going into the game, with St Rynagh's the kingpins at the time... with the likes of Barney Moylan, Paudge Mulhare and Pat Joe Whelahan setting them apart. However, on this wintry November day, Birr got one over on them, but they left it late and needed a goal from a 21-yard free from Declan Hennessy with under a minute remaining to snatch victory. On the way to victory, super-sub Eddie Nevin hit 1-1 when introduced in the second-half.

Birr had raced into an early 0-2 to 0-0 lead, with Declan Hennessy and Tom O'Shea shooting over, but with Barney Moylan lurking, they couldn't afford to get too comfortable. Moylan struck a free to the net to put St Rynagh's ahead and the scores kept coming at both ends as an intriguing final unfolded.

Birr missed some gilt-edged chances early on and they were punished when Paudge Mulhare grabbed a second goal for St Rynagh's, but the winners dug in and three frees from Joe Hernon ensured that Birr went in at half-time within striking distance, trailing 2-5 to 0-8.

St Rynagh's began to get the upper-hand in the second-half, but the introduction of Nevin changed the course of the game as, within minutes of coming on, he fired a goal and a point to leave just one point between the teams with 13 minutes to go. Mulhare kicked a point to leave two in it, before Declan Hennessy's late rocket of a free gave Birr the win and the long awaited return of the Sean Robbins Cup.

The win was anchored by their defence, with Mick Spain, who was also the team trainer, lording it at full-back. Only two St Rynagh's players scored in the game, an indicator of the huge work and determination shown by the Birr rearguard.

★★★★★

"

I HAVE A lot of games in my head.

In 1949 I was playing centre-back on the Drumcullen team that won the Offaly Minor Hurling Championship. It was the first minor team that Drumcullen ever put out, and we played Tullamore in the final. I was only 16 at the time.

I also remember playing in an All-Ireland junior hurling final in 1953 against Tipperary. I was playing in the middle of the field and Tipp had the great Theo English and Mick Kelly, who had captained Kilkenny to a senior All Ireland in 1957, but was playing junior against us that day because of something to do with him being in Tipperary with the army.

Those two were in the middle of the field against me and I remember thinking to myself in the week leading up to the game, *All I can do is go out and do my best!*

If I get the first ball, I am going to hit it the furthest I can.

I caught the first ball that came to me and, true to plan, I hit it about 20 yards wide... drove it into the crowd on the hill behind the goals. I used to often say to myself, *Why didn't I aim it at the goals?*

It turned out that I was the best man on the pitch after that. I was hitting the ball into the forwards, nice and low, but I might as well have been throwing water into the Shannon... it was a waste of time.

We only scored 1-2 in the game, and we were beaten 1-7 to 1-2. If I was to do it all again, when I had the ball in my hands I should have just hit it over the bar myself. But I was told to hit it in low.

I went on to captain Drumcullen to Offaly senior hurling titles in 1957 and '58, but those games, along with the junior All-Ireland, are trumped by Birr winning the Offaly senior hurling title in 1971.

That's the one I remember most. Birr hadn't won the championship for 20-odd years. I was brought in as the trainer even though I was playing as well.

Fr Carey came from Roscrea at the time... and Roscrea were after winning the All-Ireland club title. Before Fr Carey came to Birr, we said we would get him in as chairman of the club. I asked him would he do it, but he said no, as it could cause tension. I told him that wouldn't happen.

Then he told me that if he went for the chair, the sitting chairman would be vexed and there would be a row. Now, what I didn't tell him at the time was that I was the chairman.

Instead, I told him that the chairman wouldn't mind... still not telling him it was me. I called to him two or three times and guaranteed him the chairman wouldn't object to him.

The evening of the AGM, I visited him and asked him again, and he was still saying no but, then, he just asked me... 'By the way, who is the chairman?' I told him then that it was me. So he went in and did the job in the end.

He was able to talk to the players. I remember he came up to my house one day and asked me how training was going? I told him we had to do something with Brian Coolahan. Now, Brian Colahan was a great hurler, but another player came to me saying that Brian was giving out too much to the young lads up at training and he was going to turn lads against it.

Fr Carey suggested that if Brian was giving out to players at training the next night, that I was to call the players together... but wait until he (Fr Carey) was there and in sight. He told me to read the riot act to him, so I did, and Brian said that if that was the way I wanted it, then I can have it... and he walked off.

I saw him going up to the dressing-room and, next thing, I saw Fr Carey walking in after him. Later that night, Fr Carey came down to my house. I asked him how he got on?

Fr Carey explained that he asked Brian what was wrong? Brian told him that, 'You couldn't please Mick Spain!' Fr Carey asked Brian to promise that he would be training the next evening... and that he would read me the riot act. And we after planning this whole thing! Brian never opened his mouth after, and he was a great hurler. That was the *sports psychology* back then.

We won the county final that year... and it was a funny thing.

Declan Hanniffy got married the week before and he was the only county player on the panel. He had his honeymoon booked, and it clashed with the day of the final. So, he was missing for the final, and Declan Hennessy got married on the Friday but said he would stay for the game before going off on his honeymoon.

Hennessy scored our winning goal that day as captain.

Fr Carey came to me and told me that he could get the final put back a week or two, but I told him, 'No!' The lads knew Declan was going and there were subs raring to get in. There would only have been a row.

We brought in Eddie Nevin in place of Declan, and he scored a goal and a point… and won the match for us.

Damien Martin was in goals for St Rynagh's on the day and he picked the ball up in the penalty area during a bit of a melee, and we got a free. Declan Hennessy stuck it in the net. They were leading by two points, but that penalty saw us win by a point.

We all still meet up and have a laugh about when we were playing and what went on. That day gave me the best thrill of all. All those lads were great and I made lifelong friends from that group.

Before moving to Birr, I was hurling with Drumcullen and we were used to winning. After that final in 1971, I went home. I didn't drink, but I was delighted we won.

When I was playing with Drumcullen we won seven out of 10 titles and there were no big celebrations. Lads might have gone to a dance that night and had a bit of craic.

There were big celebrations in Birr after winning in 1971, however, and we had to play in the Leinster Championship the following week, but we were at *nothing*. I wouldn't blame lads for having a drink. If a team nowadays won a county final after 20-odd years of tying, there would be some celebrations!

I enjoyed it, because it was my first go at management. I was with Birr since 1960 so I was 11 years in the club at that stage. Having won a lot with Drumcullen, I was coming to Birr and trying to get them to train harder and I was trying to put a bit of grit into them.

They were right good hurlers. We had a half-back line that day of Joe Hernon, John Cleary and Brian Colahan. Brother Acquin and Mick Gleeson were immense too. They hurled on Pat Joe Whelahan and Dick Johnson… and held their own, and even won the battle. Pat Joe and some of them were on the county team at the time, and our boys weren't.

When I came to Birr first, we were playing Coolderry in a league game. For whatever reason, I was out on the Roscrea Road that morning and I met Brian Colahan and Patsy Pardy going up the road with a bucket of lime and brushes with them.

They were going to mark out a field for a soccer game – they played soccer earlier in the day and came running into the dressing-room for our league game.

I dropped the two of them!

They were our only two county men, but it sent out a message that I wasn't going to tolerate that kind of thing. I had nothing against soccer, and I actually said at an AGM one year when I was chairman that I hoped young lads in Birr would play GAA but if they weren't going to play that, I wanted to see them playing rugby or soccer.

I was *near ate* for saying that at an AGM, but I still hold those thoughts. So long as a young lad is playing *some* game – I would prefer if they played GAA, of course. But everyone is different.

Fr Carey was the man who kept the whole thing together. If there was something going on in the background, he would have a word and act as peacekeeper. He used to call to the houses of the players, to make sure they were alright.

You have up to 30 individuals, and they are all thinking differently... there could be problems at home... or one hundred other things going on.

I carried that train of thought through to when I was involved with Offaly. If a player was missing any night, I would pick up the phone and tell him I missed him at training... and ask if everything was alright? By just saying that to him, you had him back... because you let him know he was wanted, and that he was important.

I was with Offaly then, after that. 1980 gave me a great thrill... I never thought I would see that. Winning a Leinster final was massive, but then we won the All-Ireland in 1981, '85 and '94. I was with the management team for all of those. It was something special.

I remember we were going into Croke Park for the 1980 Leinster final and, at that time, any member of management or administrator with a team got a ticket going in... and I stuck the ticket into one of my pockets.

I was in the dressing-room. I waited until everyone was gone out in case hurls or anything were left behind. Diarmuid Healy was after giving a speech to the lads... it made the hair stand on the top of your head.

He told the lads that he seen old Offaly hurlers up in the Hogan Stand and the tears rolling down from their eyes... now, bear in mind we were over on the Cusack Stand side of the field!

Diarmuid had gone to the toilet in the dressing-room so the two of us were late enough going out on to the field, but when he came to the gate to get out of the dressing-room and on to the field, the steward wouldn't let us out… we couldn't find our tickets!

Diarmuid took a hurl out of my hand and told the steward that if he didn't let us out that he would split him. The steward said he was going to get the guards.

So, a guard came down.

Diarmuid told the steward that we were two officials with the Offaly team… and he had to let us in!

Watching Diarmuid going out on to the field, I could see he was furious. The ball had been thrown in and all, before we got out there. I thought to myself that it was bad for Diarmuid to be this wound up, because he normally wouldn't be.

I called him back, and said to him, 'You must have great eyesight!'

'WHAT DO YOU MEAN?' he replied in a raised voice.

'Look over at the Hogan Stand… I can't make out one person over there… and here are you telling us that you can see people over there with tears running down their faces.' The two of us started to laugh and the mood was lightened again.

One of the years, coming up an All-Ireland final, Diarmuid was training the team and they were having a game of 'backs and forwards'. I went up to him and told him that the subs were getting no training, that they were out on their own and all they were doing was pucking a ball around.

We thought they should have been mixed into the 'backs and forwards' game. But Diarmuid said he couldn't do that. He said he was training to win an All-Ireland! Pat Fleury and Pat Carroll used to beat the ribbons out of one another but when they went out in a game, they would hurl the very same way.

Diarmuid was a great friend and he had a great way about him.

I used to be a devil for telling lads to mark tight. I went into a dressing-room one day and told a player that he wasn't marking tight enough. The player replied that he was marking tight… that he was only a few yards from his man.

I brought him over and lay in beside him, and said, 'That's what I mean when I say tight!'

”

PAT DELANEY

KINNITTY 5-8 COOLDERRY 1-11
Offaly SHC Final Replay
St Brendan's Park, Birr
OCTOBER 28, 1979

Pat Delaney (fourth from right on the back row of the 1985 All-Ireland winning team) was a prince of centre-backs for Offaly in the 80s, but powering Kinnitty from the same position is something he can never forget.

★ **KINNITTY:** P Clendennan; M Bergin, S Kealy, Matt Corrigan; Mick Corrigan, S Clarke, G Coughlan; D Egan, J Egan; Mark Corrigan (1-5), M Cleere, **P Delaney**; J Flaherty (0-1), D Corrigan (0-1), T Carroll (3-0). Subs: B Kennedy (1-1) for Clarke, P Corrigan for Kennedy, Fr T Hannon for D Corrigan.

★ **COOLDERRY:** M Murray; L Hogan, Joe Dooley, James Dooley; M Kennedy, O Kennedy, P McLoughney (0-4); C Loughnane, T Teehan; J Teehan (0-2), P Teehan (1-0), M King; P Carroll (0-3), D Dooley (0-1), M Lyons (0-1). Subs: D Loughnane for O Kennedy, T Dooley for D Dooley.

THE ACTION

KINNITTY WERE ONCE again crowned Offaly senior hurling champions after a bumper crowd witnessed one of the best ever county finals played in St Brendan's Park, Birr.

After a draw in the first game, Kinnitty found their range in the replay with five goals sending them on their way to victory. The hurling was magical at times. Hard and fast, with very little let up as both tribes left everything on the field in the bid to claim the Sean Robbins Cup.

After being closely marshalled in the drawn game at centre-forward, Kinnitty's Pat Delaney was the stand out man on the field. After moving back to centre-back early in the game, Delaney dominated while anchoring the defence in his natural home at No 6.

The opening half was frantic stuff and the sides were level four times.

After Tom Carroll got the first of his three goals, Coolderry responded well with two frees from Pat McLoughney and a point from talisman Pat Carroll, as the gap was down to one point. Level after 15 minutes, Kinnitty edged ahead again with points from Mark and Denis Corrigan but, once again, Coolderry had the answers. Pat Teehan grabbed a goal to put them two points ahead with a couple of minutes left to half time, while another Carroll score had Coolderry looking good for a three-point half-time lead.

Kinnitty didn't read the script though and the last couple of minutes in the half saw Mark Corrigan fire 1-1 to leave them 2-7 to 1-9 ahead at half-time. In the second-half, Carroll blasted his second goal to the net, while Mark Corrigan added another point to put Kinnitty in the ascendency. The jitters came over Kinnitty for a period, but they were settled back down by Carroll's third goal after Pat Delaney and Denis Corrigan had done well in the build-up.

Eight minutes from time and Kinnitty had their fifth goal, after Brian Kennedy found the range, and Matt Corrigan went on to lift the Sean Robbins Cup, the sixth title in Kinnitty's history.

★★★★★

"

THE 1979 COUNTY final… the Kinnitty and Coolderry replay.

There was 14,000 at it in Birr… the Coolderry crowd even told me that since. I was hurling on the half-forward line, and Mick Cleere was centre-forward. Sean Clarke was playing centre-back and got his thumb broken in the first five minutes.

Cleere said to me, 'Will you go back, or will I go back?'

I went back, and I hurled for Offaly for the next 12 years at centre-back all because of that.

Mark Corrigan scored a goal in that final, just before half-time. Mick Cleere won a ball out under the flag and gave it in to Mark. He controlled it on his stick and left it on it, ran 40 yards and fired it to the net without putting it back in his hand.

There was a five or a seven-minute period in the first-half when the ball never went out over the sideline or never went wide at either end. It went from end-to-end, and I mean this was moving now… there was no quarter given anywhere.

After that spell, Mark Corrigan scored that goal and we beat them up the field then. We beat them well. Birr was a little bit tight, but you got used to it. There wasn't much carrying the ball at that time, it was all *moved.*

And the quicker you got it to the forward line, the more chance you had. Sure, it was 50-50; you pucked it down and I had a 50-50 chance, the same as you.

Give Johnny Flaherty a 50-50 ball with anyone and he will take three of them off you, out of five. He had serious upper body power. There were two Egans playing and Brian Kennedy hurling centre-half forward. He would run all day. BANG...CHOP, CHOP…PULL, BANG… he would keep going like a train.

A good few Corrigans were on that team as well… Mickey Corrigan at wing back, sweet as a nut. Mickey Bergin corner-back… Sean Clarke, a powerful man. They were all good underage players and had that confidence from winning underage.

Everybody else will have mentioned the All-Irelands and the Leinster titles, and there's nothing wrong with them either, but I thought that day in Birr… I thought I had a fantastic game in it.

Pat Carroll was hurling in his prime at that time. Jesus, there wasn't a split second in the game… a super game in that county final.

Mark Corrigan never played county senior before that day, neither did Ger Coughlan. The following Sunday, we played Tipperary in the first round of the league in Birr and both of them played for the first time.

I thought Mark Corrigan was the best forward I ever saw. If I wanted a score… if we wanted a score… Offaly or Kinnitty, if I got a ball around the half-back line, I wouldn't even look. I'd puck it up his wing… to him and Johnny Flaherty.

Flaherty would be standing 10 yards out from the goalposts and space in front of him; they knew it would be coming.

It all started when Cannon Madden came to the parish from St Flannan's after winning three Harty Cups in Ennis, and he played me centre-back all through underage; he could never understand why I wasn't centre-back for Kinnitty seniors, even in years after.

I always hurled at midfield then, as we had heaps of backs. Mick Cleere hurled centre-back, he could hurl anywhere.

Cannon Madden said you play hurling like you play soccer… down to the corner flag, and across to the 21-yard line. Take the centre-back out of it. And his policy at that time was to get the most awkward lad that you had on the team, and hurl him at centre-forward… because the best lad is always hurling centre-back for the opposition.

He was a genius at hurling, and he was very loyal to the parish. He had a huge influence in Kinnitty. He was from Clonakenny in Tipperary, and finished up in Borrisokane.

He shot pheasants, foxes, worked for the people, got on with everyone in the parish and moving the ball was his thing. We were good at moving it anyway, but by God, he drilled it home. That's where all that ground hurling came from. We had a style known to ourselves.

But that county final in particular... like, all of Tipperary came to the county finals in Offaly. Birr was the home of it at that time. But we won everything underage in Birr. We knew it inside-out, and there was a wonderful atmosphere.

At that time, it was hard to win county finals in Offaly. Coolderry were a very hard team to beat in a final. I thought that game was a huge turning point.

1980 was a great year too, when we won the first Leinster with Offaly. Did we think we would win going? Not at all. Johnny Flaherty's experience was wonderful at that time as well. He was 28 or 29 and he loved Croke Park. He had been in Croke Park 10 years previously in 1969, when they lost the Leinster final.

1981 was great as well, winning the All-Ireland, but one of my biggest regrets was '82. We had a better team that year.

We had three matches to play. We played Laois in a great match in Croke Park… a draw, and I wasn't centre-back. They played me corner-back. Martin Cuddy broke Aidan Fogarty up. But the next day, I was back out centre-back in the replay. We beat them, and beat them well.

We had to go back the following Sunday to play a Leinster final and the edge had gone off us a bit. Both sets of backs were on top… very low scoring, beaten by a point or two with a controversial goal. The ball had gone wide and it came back into play. But we should have been gone clear.

We were the better team and Kilkenny won two All-Irelands as a result of that.

We didn't get back to the All-Ireland until 1984. That day was all wrong here before we left. Preparation was all wrong.

We made a dog's dinner of it. We played Westmeath in a challenge game the previous Sunday to try and pick some of the forward line… and Westmeath turned up with 10 or 12.

The day of the game, we went to the Anner Hotel in Thurles, but we should have gone to Birr, and we should have left Birr in a bus.

I was working in Cork the following year in 1985 and didn't come back up to train, but the s***e was trained out of the team. We played Kilkenny in the semi-final in Croke Park; it was a draw. The rest of them were stuck to the ground, but I probably had the greatest game I ever had.

I had a pain in my arm pucking it up the field.

I knew I wasn't as fit as the rest of them, so I said I'd let it off when I got it. The ball followed me around Croke Park. No matter where I was, this thing was coming and I'd let it off to the far end… and it would come back again.

Joachim was moved to centre-forward after half-time and he destroyed Ger Henderson that day. We beat them by nine in the replay. We came from nine down to draw it the first day… *and beat them by nine in the replay.* That was some turnaround. Croke Park was the most beautiful place to be in June and July. The ground was like a carpet above at that time. We loved Croke Park. If you couldn't play up there, you couldn't play anywhere.

But it all started back with the parents at home. They would leave the hay in the field to bring us to underage matches. If Father Madden said it, you did it.

He would often bring us to matches. He had a Volkswagen and we were going to an under-14 match one day. There were three in the front, and I was in the middle changing the gear stick. There were two behind the back seat... and he had five across the back seat itself. JIE 477 was the registration number of it.

One of the big things that Diarmuid Healy brought that other managers maybe didn't was that he left you fresh. The last big training session was nine days out on the Friday before the match. We would have a match on the Sunday and a puck around on the Tuesday or Wednesday.

It was a glorious era and when the All-Irelands were won that time, The County Arms in Birr was where everyone went. The old people all came in from the rural parishes and they all parked on their own road. They all knew where they were and they would all go home after it.

Who got the biggest thrill out of winning the Leinster titles and All Irelands in the 80s? I worked with the Department of Agriculture and was out with the farmers, the old people. They thought they'd never see it.

The people had never seen success before 1981... and to see what it meant to them. They all came out to welcome us home. Sure, they didn't *go home.* There was no rush to go home. No guards bothered... no one bothered. They guided you all home that time. They were wonderful times.

How we didn't win an All-Ireland club at the time is a mystery. We were beaten in three Leinster club finals in-a-row. Ballyhale Shamrocks beat us in one, Muckalee beat us and they went and won the All Ireland. Buffers Alley beat us in the next one.

We won three county titles in-a-row, but when it got to the Leinster stage, the conditions didn't suit our style of hurling. We were a top of the ground team and that was probably a big factor in it. The ball got bogged down.

The great Offaly minor teams came in the late 80s and look what they did!

They will all tell you the hurling in Birr was down to Brother Denis in the college, but Brother Vincent in the national school was a big part too.

Birr won the colleges' All-Irelands, but they had some ammunition. For a small school like it, it was some achievement. To come with the stick-men they had and to go take on St Kieran's… to take on the whole lot of them? They were super games.

They were super hurlers.

Was Brian Whelahan the best? I thought he was the best I've seen anyway. I thought he had the greatest pair of feet. I think he could have hurled anywhere; he was that good.

Jimmy Barry Murphy told me that when Cork beat Offaly in the semi-final in 1999, Cork had sixty-five percent possession, and Offaly still led at half-time. Whelahan… every ball he let up the field, he pucked it in perfectly. Genius.

I thought Martin Hanamy was a super corner-back. If you were going to war in the morning, you would bring him with you. Under that gate in Birr… Hanamy's corner, as I called it. Charlie Carter told me at a camogie match in Birr, four or five years ago… he said, 'This was a fortress… imagine hurling here on Hanamy… trying to get a score?'

Hanamy was ball, man and all… a wonderful hurler.

Offaly got everything out of everyone they had at the time. I don't think we would have survived today with the bigger panels. If any man got injured, we were gone. *No one* got injured.

It took three matches to win an All-Ireland in 1981. Look at how many matches it would take to win an All-Ireland now. You were fresher, and there was a better appetite for it.

I have a fierce love affair with the pitch in Birr. Under-12, under-14, under-15 and under-16 finals all won there in the mid-60s.

Kinnitty came with a rare good underage team and they all came through. I won under-14 finals with my brothers, and Kinnitty hadn't won anything for 30 years.

We won the junior county title in 1966 and the senior in '67. The club went straight from junior to winning a senior the following year. I was carrying the Lucozade… my God, the memories.

”

PAT FLEURY

OFFALY 3-17 KILKENNY 5-10
Leinster SHC Final
Croke Park
JULY 13, 1980

Pat Fleury gathers the ball in his own defence during the historic Leinster final win over reigning All-Ireland champions Kilkenny in 1980.

★ **OFFALY:** D Martin: P McLoughney, M Kennedy, **P Fleury**; A Fogarty, P Delaney (0-1), G Coughlan; J Kelly, B Keeshan; M Corrigan (0-4), B Bermingham (1-2), P Carroll; P Kirwan (0-4), P Horan (0-6), J Flaherty (2-0). Subs: E Coughlan for Fogarty, M Cashen for Kelly.

★ **KILKENNY:** N Skehan; J Henderson, B Cody, D O'Hara; R Reid, G Henderson, N Brennan; J Hennessy (0-1), F Cummins; G Fennelly (0-1), J Wall (0-1), K Fennelly (0-1); M Brennan, B Fitzpatrick (1-5), M Ruth (3-1). Subs: L O'Brien for Cummins, M Crotty (1-0) for K Fennelly, M Kennedy for Brennan.

THE ACTION

HISTORY WAS MADE in Croke Park as Offaly claimed a first ever Leinster senior hurling title in dramatic fashion over a fancied Kilkenny side. Despite conceding five goals, including a hat-trick from Matt Ruth, Offaly had the mental and physical toughness to overcome their old rivals.

A paltry crowd of around 9,000, however, was in attendance to witness Padraig Horan raise the Bob O'Keefe Cup. It was a win that not many people saw coming, typified by the small crowd, but after the opening exchanges in the game the Offaly men made sure that Kilkenny knew they were in a game.

They blitzed Kilkenny early on and led 1-6 to 0-2 after 13 minutes, with the goal coming from Johnny Flaherty, one of only two survivors from their last Leinster final appearance in 1969, along with goalkeeper Damien Martin.

Kilkenny settled into the game though and in Matt Ruth, they had a man on top of his art. He found the net towards the end of the opening quarter, before Billy Fitzpatrick blasted home a penalty to suddenly turn the game on its head. After making such an impressive start that saw Offaly lead by seven points after 13 minutes, the winners would go in trailing 3-6 to 1-10 at half-time after Ruth grabbed his second goal just before the break.

There was nothing between them in the second-half. A Mark Corrigan point put Offaly in front with 18 minutes to go, but Kilkenny once again struck back with three in-a-row before a goal from Brendan Bermingham on 57 minutes levelled the game for the last time.

The defining score landed three minutes later when Flaherty gathered a Padraig Horan delivery and found the net.

Horan landed his sixth point of the day to put his side four points up with four minutes to play, and although Ruth completed his hat-trick in the closing stages, Offaly held on to win by a point.

★★★★★

"

IF YOU LOOK at Offaly hurling, we got to three Leinster finals in 1924,'26 and '28. That was incredible and it shows that hurling in Offaly was obviously very strong at the time.

We didn't manage to win any of those finals, but we did win two Junior All-Irelands in the 1920s. Then emigration decimated us. We went into a dark period and it wasn't until Bord na Mona and the ESB came along that things started to improve.

From my own personal experience of it all, I am brought back to that great team we had in 1969, that lost out so narrowly... the only problem was half of them were well into their thirties, and the other half were in their early twenties.

It was heartbreak to lose that Leinster final. Kilkenny were so good and so dominant but here we were taking them on. It didn't go our way, but who would think that 11 years would pass by before we were in another Leinster final.

We had two survivors from back then in Damien Martin and Johnny Flaherty, and both of them played very significant roles in getting over the line... even if Johnny did spend a lot of time out of the country.

He came back at a very good time. A lot of the older lads from that 1969 final retired in the years after and sometime in the mid-70s, it was decided to bring in a new wave of younger guys.

Joachim Kelly and myself were brought on board around 1975, and then Pat Delaney came and, little by little, there was a new set of faces. In the late-70s, our priority was the league and it had to be. With all the optimism in the world, we didn't see ourselves winning Leinster and All-Ireland titles but if we could get up to Division 1A, well then, we would be testing ourselves against the top teams.

In the 1975-76 league we were in Division 1B, and we beat Westmeath and Kildare but lost to Limerick, Antrim and Waterford, so that wasn't a massively impressive campaign. The 1976-77 league was when we got promoted. That was the year of the famous league game against Wicklow, where we beat them 0-3 to 0-1. Thankfully, there is no footage of that game doing the rounds.

We also beat Laois, Kildare, Galway and Antrim, and drew with Waterford, to top the group before going out in a quarter-final to Wexford.

Now we were there in the top division... and we had to stay there. There was no point going up and down every year.

In 1977-78, we won three and lost three. We beat Wexford, Galway and Cork, while losing to Kilkenny, Clare and Tipperary. We ended up in the relegation play-off that year against Cork in Thurles.

We beat them and they went on and won the All-Ireland, so maybe we did them a favour and gave them a toe in the rear-end. We took as much out of that relegation play-off so it is all relative.

The following year we won two, drew two and lost two. One of our wins was against Kilkenny, and that was significant for what was to come down the line. I remember beating Galway in various league games. We beat them in Ballinasloe and Loughrea, but they kept bringing us further and further west so, the third time we beat them, we were in Salthill.

The usual pleasantries were being exchanged after the match and the Galway officials came into the dressing-rooms wishing us well and telling us that they would see us next year. Paudge Mulhare stood up and said to them, 'The way things are going, ye will be bringing us to the Aran Islands next year'.

In the league in 1979-80 we beat Kilkenny again, in Nowlan Park. We beat Limerick, drew with Tipperary and lost to Clare in Galway. That was the year of the infamous game with Clare in Tulla. It was one of the most extraordinary occasions I was ever involved in.

How what happened even came about is still hard to explain.

Clare were doing up Cusack Park at the time, so they were using Tulla and winning. It became known as 'Fortress Tulla'.

It was a great match. A hard, tough, but clean league game. But when the final whistle blew a row broke out. We found ourselves all getting sucked into it... it was serious stuff. Pat Carroll was brought into the dressing-room after getting a bad belt. I remember going in the dressing-room door and, just as I was turning in the door, something touched the back of my hair.

A rock, about half the size of a football, crashed in smithereens against the far wall. I went to head back out the door and, thank God, somebody grabbed me because the first fella I met was going to get something and it wasn't going to be a pat on the back.

It took ages before everyone got into the dressing-room.

The room was packed. The guards and the ambulance were brought out, and the Clare supporters never went home. They stayed there.

We were making our way to the bus and there were Clare people there... 10 deep on either side of the bus. They left us an avenue to walk through and it wasn't six feet wide. We took a look out the door at the avenue that the stewards and guards had made for us... and anyone who had helmets went back in, and put them on.

We were togged in at this stage. If you had a girlfriend or a wife, you had her by one hand, the hurl in the other hand. We walked out and there wasn't a sound.

It was so eerie.

If anyone had to say or do anything... it all could have kicked-off again.

There was a big investigation and loads of us were brought up to answer questions. Of course, nobody saw *anything*... there was massive blindness and amnesia around it. We were told to play all our league games away from home the following year, a massive punishment at that stage of our development.

It was the best thing that ever happened to us, however. We played every game away from home and ended up getting to a league final, losing to Cork, but no one was going to worry about losing a league final the following July. That pulled us together even more.

On to 1980, and we got a hard game from Laois in the first round – 2-10 to 0-12 – and beat Dublin in the semi-final, 0-18 to 0-10.

There were two things that really pleased us about the Leinster final – the fact that we scored 3-17, and unusually that Kilkenny only scored 10 points. Now we wouldn't have been happy with them scoring five goals but, on the day, Matt Ruth was just having one of those games; he got three goals. The selectors moved Pat McLoughney out to the wing, and put Aidan Fogarty back in on him, but he was just on his game and when a forward gets a day like that, it doesn't matter who is marking him.

Diarmuid Healy was enticed into the fold at the end of 1979. There was no way in the world that he would have expected to have us winning a Leinster final six months later. We never really thought about the fact that we hadn't won one before.

Diarmuid was very good at getting your heads right.

He had plenty of information on the Kilkenny team, and he convinced us that this was a possibility... we could win it. That, allied to the fact that we had only lost to Wexford by a point in the semi-final the year before, gave us a great boost.

We were 1-6 to 0-2 ahead after about 15 minutes... Johnny Flaherty got the goal. The crowd was so small but we weren't aware of that. The one thing Diarmuid stressed to us was to not look up at the crowd during the parade. We were staring at the back of the neck of the lad in front.

Now, he didn't realise that there would only be around 9,000 people there!

They came back and got a few goals, and we ended up going in at half-time two points down. We went from seven points up... to a few points down. Yet, there was no negativity in the dressing-room. Nobody thought our chance was gone.

We had a positive chat amongst ourselves.

Diarmuid came back in with a big smile on his face. He told us he was delighted with how things had gone. He told us that we had proved in the first 15 minutes that we were well able to hurl them off the field... he covered all the bases.

I had no doubts that we were going to make a war out of the second-half. They went a point or two up, and then we came back... they came back, we replied... and so on. Matt Ruth seemed to get a goal every time we got close.

Kilkenny took off Frank Cummins. Now, Frank was the king of midfielders, strong as a horse. He hadn't his best half, but I have no doubt that if he was left on he would have come into the game in the last 20 minutes. He came back in 1982 and '83 and won two All-Irelands from the middle of the field in his mid-thirties.

They brought in Chunky O'Brien, but Chunky was going off the boil around then. Brendan Bermingham got 1-2 for us that day. You will hear so many tributes about Brendan from our group. If ever the word selfless was made for someone, it was him. The hardest working centre-forward in the world.

I ran into Ger Henderson coming out of the 1984 Munster final in Thurles. We had a chat and he told me to tell Brendan that he was asking for him. 'That man broke my heart', he said. '1-2 in the Leinster final in 1980!' said Ger, shaking his head.

Brendan got a great goal that day. Padraig Horan took a free and it was blocked on the line, but Brendan followed in and kicked it straight into the net...

and got a couple of clatters for his troubles. Shortly after that, we got our next goal. Joachim got a bad head injury and the ball dropped out to the wing. Padraig Horan sent in a lovely ball and Johnny Flaherty got it... and got the goal.

There were still about 10 minutes left at that stage. Kilkenny came back and got another goal, but it was unique that Kilkenny only get 10 points... and that was a sign of our defence. Any bit of lead we had in that second-half was tested, especially in the last 15 minutes. We were playing the All-Ireland champions in a Leinster final... and we had never won one. If any one of the lads kind of folded or had any doubts, it was going to be curtains... it was that tight.

I remember coming out with one ball, and I got upended.

For fear I was going to get up, the lads on the sideline came in and were nearly kneeling on my chest getting me to stay down. I was anxious to get up, but they were trying to get me to stay down. It was a bit of gamesmanship.

The big fear at the end was that Kilkenny would get another goal, because they had got five already. There must have been a bit of panic from Kilkenny, however. They didn't finish the game the way they normally play. They were normally very good to open up the play, but they went back to a straight forward game and that helped our defence. The last thing we needed was Kilkenny creating space and opening up gaps. Thank God, we got over the line. There is a great shot near the end of the game... Ger Henderson is driving a ball in from a '65', I think.

The Walshes lived up between Drumcullen and Kilcormac, and Leo Walsh had a pub in Birr. Leo was in the stands... and he appears on the screen. Ger is leaning over the free and the camera shoots up to the stands, and there is Leo with the hands over his face... almost peeking out through his fingers.

He would have seen Offaly play and come close in the past, and he was probably praying that we could squeeze one more minute out of it. And saying decades of the rosary! I was shattered after it. To see lads who had played in games like the 1969 Leinster final, the likes of Willie Gorman, and Paddy Molloy, our own hero in Drumcullen. To meet those lads on the pitch after... they were as excited as we were!

Johnny Flaherty added a whole new dynamic to the forward line with his brains and leadership. Padraig Horan had hurled centre-back in previous years, but was now at full-forward, with Pat Delaney at centre-back.

The year that the selectors chose to put Ger Coughlan on the panel, I was convinced we were going in the right direction. It was one of the better things that a selection committee has done – to have the conviction to pick a guy, irrespective of his size, just purely his skill levels.

He was hurling personified. He was *all skill*. He had no business trying the other stuff because he wasn't big enough, but he would take a ball out of your eye. I had the pleasure for years of playing behind him and, in my own mind, to *mind* him… but sure he was well able to mind himself.

It was amazing that when it was won, we couldn't have had a better captain than Padraig Horan. If ever there was a fella that encapsulated guts and leadership! He would go through hell and back. He could have been involved with the footballers in the 1970s but, without blinking an eye, he went with the hurling.

His father passed away at home during the match, and I remember I was reeling after hearing the news. What an awful thing to happen on this day of all days, and especially to our captain. Tommy Horan was a fierce GAA man and as tough as nails. Padraig didn't take it from the ground. The Kilkenny lads came up to the funeral and that was very well received. Tommy was buried on a Tuesday and, typical Padraig, he was back training with us on the Thursday night.

JOACHIM KELLY

OFFALY 3-20 LAOIS 6-10
Leinster SHC Semi-Final
Croke Park
JUNE 21, 1981

Offaly manager Joachim Kelly celebrates with his daughter, and Offaly player, Aoife after the 2009 All-Ireland Junior Camogie Championship final in Croke Park, where the midfielder enjoyed so many brilliant days himself.

★ **OFFALY:** C King; T Donohue, M Kennedy, P Fleury; A Fogarty, P Delaney, G Coughlan; **J Kelly**, L Currams (0-2); M Corrigan (1-5), B Bermingham (0-1), P Kirwan (0-2); P Carroll (0-5), P Horan (2-2), J Flaherty (0-1). Subs: S O'Meara for Kennedy, D Owens (0-2) for Bermingham.

★ **LAOIS:** M Kelly; J Doran, J Bohane, J Ring; C Jones (2-0), J Delaney, A Lanham; M Cuddy, M Walsh (0-3); B Bohane (2-3), M Cuddy (1-1), M Brophy (0-1); P Critchley, PJ Cuddy (1-2), T Flynn. Subs: J Killeen for Ring, F Keenan for Critchley

THE ACTION

A GAME FOR the ages as the Leinster Championship sprung into life in Croke Park, with reigning provincial champions Offaly just about scraping over the challenge of Laois.

Offaly and Laois hadn't met in Croke Park since 1898 despite their fierce and close rivalry, but this one will go down as one of the most extraordinary games ever witnessed at GAA headquarters.

The first of the nine goals arrived as early as the opening minute, when Christy Jones blasted a penalty to the net. Laois had the Offaly defence in all sorts of trouble but a 17th minute goal from the stylish Mark Corrigan settled the champions and put them into a two-point lead.

Laois were unfazed and hit back with two goals in the space of a minute – Martin Cuddy with the first, and a Billy Bohane free from all of 70 metres which went all the way to the net.

As the drama unfolded, Padraig Horan's effort at goal was eventually given as a goal despite one umpire originally signalling wide, and the Laois lead was cut to 3-9 to 2-8 at half-time.

Intent on putting things right, Offaly roared out of the traps in the second-half and levelled the game but were hit again by Laois, this time PJ Cuddy reacting quickest to find the net after a line-ball had come back off the post.

Despite hitting 11 second-half wides, Offaly took to the front when Horan found the net for the second time to put them 3-18 to 4-10 up with five minutes to go. However, a second penalty from Jones was followed by Billy Bohane sending a '65' all the way to the net and now Laois were up by one.

There was more drama to come as Pat Carroll landed a sensational equaliser, before Paddy Kirwan nailed the winning score from a free on his own half-back line.

★★★★★

"

FOR ME, IT'S the memory of the whole day. A score of 6-10 to 3-20.

There were nine goals scored that day... imagine scoring six goals and not winning the game?

Cheddar Plunkett, who is now the Laois manager, said after the game that it was the start of Offaly and the fall of Laois. If they had won that game they could have gone on and won the All-Ireland like we did.

I met him after the game; he was gutted and he said that we would probably go on and win the All Ireland – and we did. Pat Critchley wrote in his book as well that it was the most disheartening game he ever played in.

It was knockout back then too. It was in June... 31,000 at the game, with Kilkenny and Wexford playing in the other semi-final.

Billy Bohane got 2-3, PJ Cuddy scored 1-2 and Christy Jones scored two goals for Laois. We had Padraig Horan with 2-2, Mark Corrigan 1-5... and Liam Currams was brilliant in midfield.

Our goalkeeper Christy King got fierce flak that day, but it wasn't his entire fault. He was replaced the next day. Most of the balls that were dropped into the square that day... there was very little he could do about them.

We should have been gone. Padraig Horan got a goal that went in through the side-netting. It was definitely wide. The umpire put the flag up, but he didn't know if it was a goal or not. Johnny Flaherty shouted 'GOAL''... and a roll of toilet paper came streaming across the goals. Laois didn't protest either.

The previous May, we beat them in a league semi-final in Nowlan Park. They had beaten Tipperary to get to the semi-final. Another cracker of a game... there was about 15,000 at it. Aidan Fogarty got sent off and we won it by four or five points in the end. Cork beat us in the league final after. It was an awful day. Cork played with the wind in the first-half, but when we came back out after half-time to play with the wind, it had gone calm.

The last three minutes of the game against Laois in Croker, I played it down with the referee John Denton. I asked John how long was left? He said a minute or two... and we were a point down. Christy King pucked out the ball and Pat Carroll caught it... and put it over the bar off his left.

It was the most famous score he ever got. I know he got a goal in the All-Ireland final a few months later but that point was his most important. If he didn't get that fantastic score to draw it, we wouldn't have won the All Ireland.

I said to Denton, 'Blow it up and we'll have a replay!' But the ball was pucked out by Laois. We won a free.

Paddy Kirwan took the free from about 100 yards. I was in Denton's ear again, telling him to blow it up. He said he would blow it up when it dropped, but sure it dropped over the bar. He gave them one more chance despite me telling him to blow it up, but they didn't get a score, thank God.

We were keeping in touch with points. We nullified their goals with points. Mark Corrigan with five and Pat Carroll with another five, so that was 10 points straightaway. Every time they got a goal, we came back and got a few points.

We went five points ahead at one stage in the second-half but they came back with a couple of goals. It was an extraordinary game. We drew with them the following year, and beat them in a replay. There was never anything between us and Laois in those days. They were a fine team.

We stopped in Edenderry on the way home and went into Paddy McCormack's pub. It was the first year of *The Sunday Game*. We had a great night.

We were aiming to win an All-Ireland. If you won the Leinster Championship that time, you were in the All Ireland-final. There was great incentive to get through Leinster. We had four matches to win an All-Ireland... Dublin, Laois, Wexford and then Galway in the All-Ireland final later that year.

My memory of the Leinster final against Wexford was Tom Donoghue knocking out Tony Doran halfway through the first-half with an awkward stroke. Doran had to be carried off and we only beat them by two points. If Tony had still been on the field, he could have been the difference – small margins again.

Within the space of a few weeks, we had beaten Laois in a controversial game and then beat Wexford in the final. It is hard to believe it is 41 years ago. We are all getting the wrong side of 65.

You will notice that I didn't pick the 1981 All-Ireland final.

I hardly hit a ball in that game. I only had about six possessions in the whole game that day. The very first ball landed down between Aidan Fogarty and PJ

Molloy. Aidan was brilliant at grabbing the ball and we had this understanding together; we played on the same side of the field.

I drifted over to take a pass off Aidan, but Molloy caught the ball and threw it out to Steve Mahon, who I should have been marking and he put it over the bar. That upset me a bit and we ended up just trying to mark each other.

I loved playing midfield. You had space to roam, and I was fierce fit at the time. I was up and down the field and would have covered a lot of ground. I was working in the Guards in Templemore in the Physical Education side of things and the 80s and the early 90s were the best years of my life.

We won so much; we played in 11 Leinster finals... winning seven. I played in three All-Ireland finals and won two of them.

Padraig Horan was a great leader... a real man. He was someone I always looked up to. You would have been more afraid of Horan at half-time than Diarmuid Healy.

I came on in the mid-70s and we were holding our own with teams around the country. We were in Division 1B for a few years, but in 1977 Andy Gallagher got us together before the league – we were now in Division 1A – and he asked us were we going to commit or were we going to just come training the odd night.

We all made up our minds that year that we were going to knuckle down. We had a nucleus of a good team that year and we got to a league semi-final where we lost to Clare, who won the league.

Diarmuid Healy arrived in 1980 as a coach and he was more or less the manager the following year. He was the main man when he came in, in 1980. Andy Gallagher had done great work there but we needed someone to bring us over the line and convince us that we were as good as anyone. A Kilkenny man has only two arms and two legs the same as anyone.

We made the breakthrough in 1980 and '81 but I thought we had a better team in '82. Kilkenny beat us in the Leinster final.

We were two points up, with time up, and Kilkenny got a goal to beat us. The ball was gone wide... Damien Martin let it off, but a Kilkenny man tipped it back in to Matt Ruth, who found the net and the goal stood. That was very disheartening. We would have won the All-Ireland that year, I think.

Fine margins, but we came out the right side of decisions too over the years.

I was doing my Leaving Cert in June 1974 and, a couple of days before we were due to do the exams, Brother Denis said to me that I was going into the Offaly senior panel. We were at a prefab at the Christian Brothers School in Birr and I thought it was the greatest news I ever heard. We played Antrim in my first league game, and I scored a point.

I was 38 in 1993 when that other great Offaly team was coming at that stage. I packed it in at the end of 1993. The last action I had in an Offaly jersey was marking DJ Carey when I went in corner-back. I had started on John Power against Kilkenny in that Leinster final of 1993 and they beat us with a late goal.

Another game we should have won... and they went on and won the All-Ireland. I knew my legs were gone even though I held DJ for the 15 minutes I was on him. I was holding on to him by the jersey. He scored nothing, but I knew my time was up.

I could have probably stayed on the following year and been a sub, but that was it.

Winning the county final with Lusmagh in 1989 was unbelievable as well. We had no trainer and no manager. Our first league game was against Shinrone out in Lusmagh and we all just met before the game. We had no dressing-rooms. We were in the hall and some of the players asked if Jim Troy and myself would go out and pick a team.

We picked the team and we won.

The following league game was against Kinnitty, and we won that too. The lads said then that we should stay at it and we did. I got a selector that would be on the sideline, because myself and Jim were playing. Aidan Larkin did that job and it was a great year.

We beat St Rynagh's in the championship semi-final and it was the toughest game I ever played in. I was marking Michael Duignan for the whole hour and he was probably 10 years younger than me. We played Clareen in the final, and John 'Ginger' Kelly got a goal with the last puck of the game to win it by a point.

We drank the Anglers Rest out of it that night... but they had it stocked up again the next day.

”

DAMIEN MARTIN
(GER COUGHLAN, LIAM CURRAMS & MARK CORRIGAN)

OFFALY 2-12 GALWAY 0-15
All-Ireland SHC Final
Croke Park
SEPTEMBER 6, 1981

Damien Martin during the All-Ireland semi-final in 1984 against Galway at Semple Stadium.

★ **OFFALY: D Martin**; T Donohue, E Coughlan, P Fleury; A Fogarty, P Delaney (0-5), **G Coughlan**; J Kelly, **L Currams (0-2)**; P Kirwan, B Bermingham, **M Corrigan**; P Carroll (1-1), P Horan (0-2), J Flaherty (1-1). Subs: B Keeshan for Donohue, D Owens (0-1) for Kirwan.

★ **GALWAY:** M Conneely; S Coen, N McInerney, J Cooney; S Linnane, S Silke, I Clarke; M Connolly (0-1), S Mahon (0-2); F Gantley, Joe Connolly (0-8), PJ Molloy (0-1); B Forde, John Connolly, N Lane (0-3). Subs: F Burke for Gantley, P Ryan for Forde.

THE ACTION

OVER 71,000 PEOPLE witnessed history in Croke Park as Offaly claimed their first ever All-Ireland senior hurling title with a three point defeat of reigning champions Galway.

Despite trailing by six points at half-time, the Offaly men roared back into the game and a goal three minutes from time by Johnny Flaherty proved the defining score. In a repeat of the 1980 All-Ireland semi-final, Offaly got the job done this time as Croke Park descended into a sea of green, white and gold upon captain Padraig Horan lifting the Liam MacCarthy Cup.

The man-mountain centre-back, Pat Delaney opened the scoring for the Faithful County to settle any first final nerves, but Galway were quick to react and regain control. Offaly were playing against the wind but were given a massive shot in the arm when Pat Carroll rattled in their first goal after Flaherty had done superbly in the build-up.

Galway regained the lead with Joe Connolly to the fore and it took a sensational save from Damien Martin to keep Offaly within touching distance. At half-time, it was the Tribesmen who went in leading, 0-13 to 1-4.

Galway went seven points up early in the second-half but, slowly but surely, Offaly began to eat into the lead as they sprung to life. Delaney nailed another long range free, and with five minutes to go Carroll and Flaherty combined once again for the latter to stylishly fire over and leave it a two-point game coming down the home stretch.

With three minutes to go, Croke Park erupted as Offaly found their second goal. A sweeping move saw them race up the field before Kinnitty's Flaherty, with his back to goal, hand-passed to the net. A shell-shocked Galway could only look on in disbelief and their misery was compounded when substitute Danny Owens and Horan added the insurance scores.

★★★★★

"

IN 1964 WE played Westmeath in the first round of the minor championship in Tullamore, and the same day I was a sub goalkeeper for the senior team in the Leinster Championship as well. I went into the senior dressing-room and, while Offaly were *nowhere* at the time, I was looking around at Paddy Spellman, Paddy Molloy and these lads. They were gods to me.

So I was there from 1964, still playing minor and a sub at the start, but playing most of that time until 1981... a long time.

We tasted relative success in 1980 winning the Leinster final. That was probably the biggest game, but when the game was over and we went into the dressing room, I heard that Padraig Horan's father had died during the match. Padraig was being interviewed upstairs after the match and he hadn't heard the news. I think, in the end, I had to break it to him.

That took the gloss off the whole thing to be honest but, despite the tragedy, the excitement at winning that Leinster final was unreal.

I retired after 1980. I wasn't on the team at all for the first round of the championship in 1981. Things didn't go too well for the goalkeeper and I was asked then if I would come back in. So 1981 had a fairytale element to it as well. You couldn't write it.

I have to honestly say, as I am sitting here, that if Offaly didn't win an All-Ireland, the one team I would have loved to have seen win one was Laois. We are cut out from the same cloth. When we won the All-Ireland final in 1981, we got off the train in Kingsbridge that morning and entered our own little bubble. But the last man I was talking to before that was Johnny Carroll from Camross in Laois.

Johnny was one of the best goalkeepers that I ever saw. He wished us well and I know in his heart that he really wanted Offaly to win. Then, when the final whistle went, there was a whole crowd around me... but these two lads got a hold of me and put me up on their shoulders. One of them was Tim Keenan from Camross, who hurled with Laois. The Lord of mercy on him since, but Tim would cut you in two on the field... and he often buried me. The other man was John Cox from Killeigh, who was involved with the GAA all his life. I have a shocking bad memory but I'll never forget things like that.

I was carrying hurls for the first round game in 1981 against Laois. I was behind the goals; I can't remember why I was put down there. I think it was to encourage the goalkeeper and all that. I had the hurls for the goalkeeper and the full-back line.

Padraig Horan got a goal that day and it wasn't a goal at all. The ball went in through the side netting. I remember Johnny Flaherty came in and he hit the crossbar a belt with his hurl and roared at the umpire to, 'PUT UP THAT F***ING FLAG!'

I was at the back of the goals beating two hurls together roaring the same thing... we only went on and won that game by a point. Paddy Kirwan got a long range free near the end of the match. That puck was probably about 80 yards at the time but, back then, players were not hitting the ball as far as they do now.

Typically though, it was 80 yards... but you talk to some lads now and they nearly have it gone out to a mile and a half.

We played Wexford then in the Leinster final, and I was back in goals for that. The Monday morning after the Laois game, I had a load of oil going off in a car and trailer. I had the car trailer on blocks and I backed the car into it. When I lifted the trailer to put it onto the car, my feet went from under me... I fell in under the trailer and the trailer fell on my leg.

Later that night, I got a phone call from Diarmuid Healy. I had to go into Tullamore on Tuesday to meet the lads. I was limping going in and I showed them my leg. By Wednesday morning, I was in the hospital. Mrs Coakley was the head physiotherapist at the time and the way I was looked after... talk about a miracle!

I had to go to the hospital twice a day for a week for physio, and they got me right and I played against Wexford. You couldn't make this stuff up.

We didn't have to play a semi-final that year. We were in to the All-Ireland final against Galway. Offaly's first ever All-Ireland senior hurling final.

We were shielded from the excitement of it to a degree, but there was no getting away from it locally. I look out the front window in my house in Banagher and I can see county Galway. All belonging to me are from Galway... and I was under fierce pressure at one stage to hurl for Galway.

One thing I can remember for sure is that we were very poor in the first-half.

The late Pat Carroll got a goal to keep us in it, and Pat Delaney kept us in it with frees as well. We were six points down at half-time and I would say there wasn't a man in the country that thought we had a hope.

Our manager Diarmuid Healy was great for getting our heads right. In 1980, we played Galway in the All-Ireland semi-final; Galway wiped the floor with us, but we had got back into the game in the second-half.

We were coming back hard at them and the referee blew the game up early... about two or three minutes short. We were back to being close enough to have a chance to win it.

So, we were six points down at half-time in 1981 and we could remember what happened the year before when we came back at Galway. At half-time, I was convinced we were going to win the All-Ireland. I don't know what happened to Galway. They weren't at the races in the second-half. While we were confident that we were going to dig it out, they were over-confident... they thought they had it won.

Every time I watch it back or see a clip of Johnny Flaherty's goal, I can see Mick Verney behind the goals and he jumping up and down. Mick was one of the lads who was behind the scenes for a long time... he was always involved.

Pat Delaney was brilliant with the long range frees; if he was hurling now, he would be putting them over from the full-back line.

When we got back to Tullamore... Christ, I will never forget it. We came down on the train and we got up onto a lorry just to come down through the town and I never knew there were as many people in Offaly. The crowds were unreal. We went from Tullamore back to Birr and there were bonfires at every crossroads.

I remember very little about the dressing-room after the game, but I do have a picture of my own son in the dressing-room. He was only around 10 at the time.

Our reception was in the Gresham Hotel but, to be honest, from the time the final whistle went... I can remember the two boys lifting me up, but I can't remember being on the Hogan Stand for the presentation, only for the bits I have seen on television since.

I vaguely remember the dressing-room but I will never forget the reception we got in Tullamore. Padraig Horan turned around to me and he said, 'Wasn't it worth it all now!' And I said back to him, 'It was worth it even if we never won it!'

Winning an All-Ireland is the icing on the cake, but it's not the cake.

It is only the icing. I would love to see the Mayo footballers win an All-Ireland medal... but they have all had the cake. The former Mayo footballer, James Nallen is a cousin of ours and whenever I am in Mayo I always say to them that the best footballer to ever play for Mayo was Sean Lowry. This would be in Crossmolina, in the hot bed of football... and I am always told to go 'Feck off back down to Offaly'.

The fact that I had retired earlier was probably in the selectors' heads. I was only hanging in and I was waiting for the tap on the shoulder. Then 1982 came and we had that now famous Kilkenny goal. It was sticking out a mile in the Leinster final that day that the first team to get a goal would win the match.

This ball came in to me anyway, and I shepherded it wide. It was gone about a foot over the end-line, when Liam Fennelly came in and clipped it back across the goal for Matt Ruth to tap it into the back of the net. The goal stood but in fairness to the referee, the way I had shielded the ball over the line, he might not have seen it.

While I was right in what I did, it would have been better if I had cleared the ball altogether, because I had time to clear it but I guarded it wide... the same as I was trained to do since I was under-12.

We got to the All-Ireland final again in 1984 and Cork beat us. I was a sub in 1985... Jim Troy was in the goals. Only for Jim we would never have got to an All-Ireland final.

We played Kilkenny and we drew with them. but Jim gave an exhibition that day, the likes of which has never been seen since. It was one of the best displays of goalkeeping that I ever saw.

I was unofficially the goalkeeping coach in 1985 as well while also sub goalkeeper. I was happy enough being a sub because I was halfway to being retired, where I wanted to be, but also still hurling.

I was always fierce fit. I used to run up to the sports field and when I was finished training up there, I would play a game of squash, and then run home afterwards.

I got Jim Troy membership of the St Rynagh's squash club. I was much better than him in the beginning. In squash, if one fella is a good bit better than the other lad, he could strangle you. I strangled Jim but by the time the year was over, it was 50/50.

Jim was sub goalkeeper in 1981. Actually, we had three goalies that year ,as Christy King was in there too and he played the first game against Laois. Jim was good enough to be in goals in 1981 and if he had have been in goals against Laois, I might not have my All-Ireland medal.

I was kept on as a sub in 1986. I was hurling well with the club but I said to Diarmuid Healy, 'Would you not find someone else?' But I was a good influence on Jim and I would say that was a big reason for me being kept on.

Jim broke his thumb before the Leinster final that year. I hurled the Leinster final in my forties. I was only hanging in and it was never in the selectors' plans that I would be playing... no one was expecting Jim to get injured.

I retired after that, 1964 to '86 inclusive.

My first match was against Wicklow in 1964. I was only 17 years of age... there is no way they should have put a young lad that age in goals in senior county hurling the way it was played back then. It was nearly more important to be bleeding after a game, than to be sweating.

Andy Gallagher played football for Tullamore and there was a football championship match on the same day as we were hurling Wicklow. I was sub goalkeeper anyway, but after about 10 minutes Wicklow had three goals scored... and I was put in.

I hurled out of my skin and kept a clean sheet, even if we were well beaten by Wicklow. That day, a young lad asked me for my autograph... and I couldn't believe it.

GER COUGHLAN

Ger Coughlan beats Seánie O'Leary during the All-Ireland final against Cork in Semple Stadium in 1984.

“

I WAS THERE at the start.

I saw it right through with Offaly hurling, from the 60s and 70s, and then I was part of it from the very late 70s and into the 80s, and everybody talks about what changed Offaly? What brought Offaly on in hurling… and how did it happen and everything else?

From my point of view, a lot of it would come back to what happened within the schools and the clubs at that time, particularly with us, I suppose. It was the schools that had a big bearing on it.

We won the under-12 county final in 1969. We got three games in the year and that was it. We played no practice matches or anything like that, so we just hurled, hurled… hurled non-stop up and down the street. There would have been no traffic.

Just before that, we had four, five or six really good hurlers in the club that you used to really look up to. Johnny Flaherty, Eddie Myles, Mick Cleere and Pat Spain were there, and that's only to name a few.

They were just incredible at that stage, and they were young as well. Flaherty and Myles were very young. That was creating an environment, but we weren't getting any matches. So, it was just basically still hurl, hurl and hurl at home... and hurl in every field we could. There was very little structured training done.

People don't realise it, but an awful lot of what they are trying to coach today, you learned it naturally back at that time... because you had to *exist.*

I suppose I was very small. Looking at photographs of the teams, I just looked absolutely ridiculous in the middle of it. You were reared up against big lads and you just had to survive, and you learned to survive. That kind of 'coaching' was incredibly invaluable.

At the time, we had a priest called Father Madden in Kinnitty and he was after coming from St Flannan's in Clare – he had trained Flannan's to major wins down there, and he came with a very basic structure of the way to hurl. He was brilliant at getting the best out of lads that were limited in their hurling ability. He just concentrated totally on them when he was training and he got them to play a very, very simple brand of hurling.

The Presentation Brothers in Birr was the place to be at the time, and I went in there in 1971. The reason why I went to Birr in the first place, aside from it being a relatively good school, was for the hurling.

In my first year, I arrived alongside Eugene Coughlan from Clareen; our own Tom Carroll, who was incredible at the time, and Aidan Fogarty and two or three more Banagher lads. They all came in from Banagher for one reason... to hurl. Then a couple of years ahead of us you had Pat Fleury and John Burke. Pat Carroll, Brendan Bermingham, Joachim Kelly and Ginger Kelly of Lusmagh were there... so we just had this incredible bunch of lads.

We had Brother Cronan over us and he arranged league matches every Thursday. So there was a half-day on a Thursday... and you had to hurl. It didn't matter. In the school, at the time, the rule was, when you were in first year... you had no choice. The rule was you hurled, and you played in the league matches.

After first year then, you could make your mind up if you didn't want to hurl.

I was captain of one of those teams at one stage and I remember it was seven or eight a-side, and we won the final that year in the school. Forty years later we had a reunion and I met some of the lads; they came up to me. They didn't want to hurl, they objected to hurling, they had never hurled in their lives… but they were *made* hurl.

To this day, however, they remember the matches and it was a great memory for them.

The under-14 team in Birr was usually made up of first years – who would rarely be on it – and mainly second years and third years. But that year, I think four of us… Pat Carroll, Eugene Coughlan Tom Carroll and myself made the team.

This was very unusual that you would have four or five… and then in third year, we had Pat Fleury, Ginger Kelly, Brendan Bermingham and Michael Langtry. They were very strong.

The competition only went as far as a Leinster final. We played Kilkenny teams and Wexford teams, and we just beat all before us really at that time.

Then, Brother Denis was training us when we were the senior team, and he was just absolutely incredible in relation to the way he wanted us to behave as players and the way we wanted to train, and everything else.

It was his discipline and his absolutely crazy madness for hurling. He was just incredibly focused and he was a very, very tough man in school. He was renowned for being tough… fair I thought, but very, very tough.

After we were beaten in a Leinster final against St Kieran's, he told us the following day that he wanted to meet us in school after 11 o'clock break in the science lab. All of the team came in and he was there in front of us. He went up to the top and looked down at us and said nothing. He went out, then… he left us and, sure, we didn't know what was after happening.

The following day, the same thing happened, after he told us to come in again. This time, he came in and went up to the top… and next thing, he broke down. Now, you can imagine young fellas looking at this man who was brought to tears.

That memory stuck with us in relation to his passion for the game.

I was brought onto the Offaly panel in 1978 and I didn't get any game… I didn't even play in the practice matches. I think they had decided that this lad is too small and just forget about him.

So, in the 1979 league, then, they picked a panel in August and I was gone... that was the end of me at that stage. I hadn't played under-21 for Offaly. I had played one match only at minor for the county.

At that stage, we played Coolderry in the 1979 county final; it went to a replay and it went down as one of the great county finals in Offaly. It was ferocious. I don't remember an awful lot, all I remember was they put me marking Pat Carroll.

We were playing Tipperary the following Sunday, and they brought me back on the panel and started me... after being dropped completely before that.

We went on to win the Leinster title in 1980. There was a big emphasis put on not giving away silly frees, as we had been guilty of that in previous years. This was decided by the players. If a lad got a score against us, he had to earn it.

The Leinster final of 1980 was just incredible because, as a backline, we just didn't hurl well. There was a lot conceded, but our forwards were incredible.

They were absolutely magnificent, the whole lot of them. It was the one day that it happened. We would always have a little banter with our forwards, about them and us, but that day they were the ones that really brought us home.

In 1981, it was probably the reverse, it was our backline that kind of held it together really; our forwards never stopped trying but things weren't happening for them.

We just had this thing with Galway. We played them a good few times and we got to know how to hurl them. On paper and everything else they could be better than us, but we just knew that we could handle them.

So, we had a great belief in ourselves against Galway. When we came out on the pitch, the Artane Boys' Band were playing a tune... and it just relaxed us. The tune they were playing... we kind of did our warm-up to the tune really, and we were very, very relaxed.

Diarmuid Healy had always said to us to hang in there... 'Ten minutes to go, we'll be in the match'. So, we had this fierce belief in ourselves that no matter how things were going, and no matter how badly things might be going, we were going to hang in there for the last 10 or 15 minutes... when we would go at them!

The crowd did an awful lot for us.

Offaly supporters had a sense of this. They would sense immediately that there was something happening. We might not be going great, we might be struggling, but you would hear this murmur from the stand, and you just knew this is it... the time had *arrived.*

I think that came through from the Offaly footballers in the 1970s. I would have been a big supporter of Offaly; I went to all their matches, all of their league matches and everything else. A belief that we would never die permeated through everybody watching them.

I had a long chat with Tony McTague a couple of months ago. That was exactly what I was telling him... and that they may not have even realised the effect they had on us. That belief... that became a huge part of the whole thing with us too.

In the first-half against Galway, we were under pressure, and they were doing all the pressing. We had missed a couple of goals. But they had missed points, and we knew the points they were missing were all because of us putting them under pressure.

That was the big thing that we had all the time... put them under pressure!

They will miss a lot, if you put them under pressure. If you foul them, they will put it down and put it over the bar. So, we were very, very happy at half-time, in relation to our backline, and in relation to where we were after what had happened.

I felt I'd had a very good first-half. And the next thing, I came out for the second-half and the selectors had made a change – they brought on Brendan Keeshan who was a wing back. Tom Donohue was coming off at corner-back because he was after getting a clatter in the first-half and someone needed to go into the corner.

I got landed corner-back, first time ever.

I had never hurled there for Offaly, not even in a practice match. But I got landed back in corner-back for the second-half, and I said to myself, *Jesus, what's happening here then!*

This is a different ball game altogether, completely different.

I suppose, some of what we all learned in the street-fighting, when we were playing the game back 10 or 20 years before that, was vitally important. We learned how to play in close quarters. I had some of the instinct that was required when the ball came in around the square.

One of the things I remember... Fan Larkin came up to Offaly one time, I think it was before a match against Wexford in 1979. That is what they used to do at the time, they might bring you someone… a famous hurler who might have a few words with you the night before the match.

They brought Fan Larkin to Banagher to talk to us.

He wasn't much bigger than me now, and when he was hurling he used to always hurl corner-back. I remember one thing he said was… 'The least amount of ball that you hit in the full-back line, the better off you are.

'Let it off wide, the goalkeeper is behind you.

'He will get it, or it will go wide.

'Mark your man, brush him aside… so that the ball goes wide.'

That kind of thinking always stood to me, and I had a few of those moments against Galway in the second-half.

I remember, I was landed on Noel Lane. Now, Noel Lane was absolutely lethal. He was over six foot tall, and like lightning. A couple of balls came in high, between me and him, and I remembered Fan Larkin's words in my ear… *Don't play this ball, let it run.*

I interfered with Lane, let the ball run… and it went wide. So, you weren't hitting any ball. You were hitting *no ball*, you weren't seen to be doing a whole lot… but you were stopping the opposition.

We just knew that we were definitely going to get our chance… our chance was going to come.

We knew we weren't taking our chances up to that, but we also knew they weren't scoring. We had stopped them scoring!

They had scored very, very little, and they were shooting from distance all the time. They kept shooting from distance, and they were renowned for that. If you had them under pressure shooting from distance, they were not going to score.

LIAM CURRAMS

Liam Currams in action against Laois in the Leinster semi-final in 1981 and (inset) as a member of the All-Ireland winning Offaly football team of 1982 he is presented with a medal to mark the 25th anniversary of the victory over Kerry by GAA president Nickey Brennan.

“

I CAME INTO the Offaly senior football squad in September 1979 while I was still a minor. I remember, my first match was down in Keenagh in Longford, against Galway in a challenge match, and then the following year I actually secured the left half-back spot… and I held it for three or four years.

The hurling only came by accident the following year, in 1981. I was fierce fit because Eugene McGee had upped the training with the footballers. Kevin Heffernan started off the physical, hard training way back in 1974 or ’75 – Mick O’Dwyer then came up against them and he had to up the training to beat them.

Then McGee came along in Offaly and he had to match it, or even up it further… so the physical training with the Offaly football team at that time was savage.

The whole month of March was taken up over in the field in Rhode. We were training for four solid weeks and there was no ball... just up and down a huge 10 acre field. There was an incline in that field and, I remember, Mick Lowry used to pair off with me and one of the things Tom Donohue used to do with us was... you had to get someone of equal weight and equal height to you, and carry that person as fast as you could up the hill.

Now, you wouldn't get 60 yards... and your two legs would go.

That was the intensity of the training. You went halfway up that field and there was a ditch up at the far hill, and Tom Donohue used to call it, 'You sprint to exhaustion'.

You'd have to sprint up the hill as fast as you could... you would never get up to the top because you were sprinting really hard and your legs would just buckle.

I was hurling with my club at that time, between all that.

Then Diarmuid Healy, in 1981, gave me the phone call and they called me on to the Offaly hurling panel. My first match was down in Nowlan Park against Laois, a lovely summer's day around Easter time.

We got to the league final that year. So, my second match was a league final... and I was 20 at that time. I was thrown in at the deep end but, because of the physical fitness I had from the football, it wasn't that hard. I was well able to run and the hurling came to me easy because I was a better hurler than a footballer... I always was.

I was on Tim Crowley. Jaysus, he's one of the hardest hurlers I've ever hurled against in all of my life. It was like running into a block of steel. We were well beaten.

We played Laois in the first round of the championship. Laois got six goals that day, but we scored a goal in that game that should never have been given. Padraig Horan had a great ground stroke and he hit a ferocious shot and it went into the back of the net... but it went in at the side of the net. We won that game by a point.

The training with the hurling team, it was kind of like a holiday camp for me.

Now, I don't say that in a nasty way because Diarmuid came in and training was all stick work... unbelievable. It was up and down in lines in O'Connor Park. Three or four in a line and the fellas in the middle then would have to hurl the ball on the ground... up and down.

If you were a midfielder or a forward, you were out the field. The backs would be in behind the goalposts in O'Connor Park... we were pucking for points all over the place.

The physical training up to the All-Ireland final in the hurling was only 15 minutes long; a couple of sprints, and that was it. As I've said, I was flying at that time because I was on the football team, so my fitness level was pretty sharp.

Whatever match was coming up, I went to the training for that game.

There was no hassle at all. Diarmuid Healy and Eugene McGee got on well. Healy wasn't one of these mad managers, and neither was McGee. If you wanted to play hurling, and if you were good enough to be on the two teams, it was fine. Nowadays, managers wouldn't stand for that at all.

The hurling final was first in 1981.

We got a lift into Tullamore train station on Kearns' bus. I met all of the boys in the railway station then. There were a few picked up along the road. The Birr boys would have been on the bus, and Danny Owens was picked up at the Blueball. I was probably the last or second last to get picked up.

We were pulling into the railway station, and a black cat ran across the front of the bus. I am not a superstitious person, but I always said it... it was kind of an omen. When a black cat runs across, especially if it runs across from your left to your right, it is good luck.

I never told that story to anyone.

But anyway, as luck had it, we won the game and we more or less stole it because it was crazy the amount of wides Galway had that day.

That Offaly team were serious guys to block and hook. You would never get a clean stroke. The likes of Ger Coughlan, Pat Delaney, Pat Fleury... they were all mighty men to hook you, and Galway couldn't settle.

They couldn't settle on a shot and the determination of those players never eased... to just keep going, to put a hurl or a boot in, put a finger in... put anything in, just to stop them getting a strike.

Switching Pat Delaney and Aidan Fogarty, that was a crucial move. Pat was centre half-back and they moved him over to right wing and that's where the goal at the end came from.

Pat had more freedom there on the right wing and he got that ball and soloed up, and gave it to Bermingham. That was as a result of that move. All we needed then was just one chance, and sure if you give a chance to Johnny Flaherty, he'd take it.

I was the youngest fella on the pitch, but I wasn't overawed with the occasion. It helped that I had played in the football semi-final the year before and there was a huge crowd in Croke Park, and I played in big Leinster finals as well.

I was marking Michael Connolly. He pulled the hurl out of my hands a couple of times going for balls. I remember in the second-half, he was doing it again and I told him that I would take his head off if he did it one more time. I wasn't actually going to take his head.

In the three games that Offaly won to win that All-Ireland, I scored two points in each match, so I contributed a small bit.

Johnny Flaherty and I used to get on well. I used to admire his skill… he had great hands, it was unbelievable what he could do with the hurling stick… great control, left or right, just a great hurler. But we would always be talking.

He was the oldest and I was the youngest, but we get on very well. Before the All Ireland final in 1981 he was over in Galway and, at that time, he was just getting going making hurleys. He was with a former Galway hurler who made the sticks and Flaherty went over to him and said, 'Have you got anything, any good sticks?' They opened the boot of the car and Johnny looked in, and went through them all, and he picked out a good stick. And he said to your man, 'I know who this stick is for!'

So, the next session, he came into O'Connor Park, and he said, 'Currams, come over here!' I went over to him anyway and he said, 'Here's a stick for you, try it out'. Honest to God, the stick was unreal.

Anything I did with that hurling stick, it went over the bar. It was long now… I liked it longer, and it was a thick handle. Flaherty knew that.

I scored a point about 10 minutes into that game. Ger Coughlan threw me out a ball and I said to myself, *If it comes out now, I'm not going to catch it… I am going to double on this ball.* Now, it was about 90 or 100 yards out, and I just doubled on the ball, and it went clean over the bar.

I wouldn't be able to do that with another stick. It was a little bit of skill as well, but it was mostly to do with the hurling stick.

I gave the hurl to John Keane, the principal of the Vocational School in Kilcormac for years. A Clare man, he was the principal when I went there.

The hurl got lost, but wait until you hear what happened.

Dan Currams, my nephew, went on and trained to be a schoolteacher and he did teaching practice in that school. There was a teacher in the school called Mr Foley, and he spotted someone taking it out of John Keane's office one day and got it back.

He had a notion who owned it, or at least the significance of it.

He kept it in his room for years. When Dan came in to do teaching practice, he called him in and he said, 'Dan, will you do me a favour and ring your uncle Liam, and ask him does he know what happened to the hurling stick he played with in that final?'

Dan made the phone call to me anyway and I said, 'As far as I know Dan, I gave it to the school in Kilcormac... but I think it was lost'.

I got them to send me a picture of it.

I knew once I saw it. So, I got it back after about 30 years. I gave it to the chairman of our club and it's in our clubhouse in Kilcormac now.

There were three weeks between the hurling and football finals.

We were in The Gresham Hotel on O'Connell Street on the night of the hurling final. That was a mad night after we won it.

They had to close the gates of the hotel... the staff opened up bars all over the place, and the place was swamped.

I don't know if we even went to bed at all; it's a bit of a blur. The next morning, we went to Tullamore. I went home to see my mother and father on the Tuesday, and that evening I went back to O'Connor Park to train with the footballers.

We got a round of applause when we went into the dressing-room... myself and Tom Donohue. Tom was on the hurling team as well and he trained the football team, the physical end of it. That was the night where I was totally focused on the football, trying to stop Kerry going for five in-a-row.

We had played Kerry in the semi-final the year before and I was conscious of the fact that I would be marking Ger Power again, so I didn't want to miss training that much. Power was hard to mark, and you had to be on your game with Power because he was so fast.

My whole ambition growing up was to play hurling for Offaly. That was my dream because I liked hurling better and I was better at it, but Eugene McGee came on the scene and he changed that.

I used to drive McGee to training from north Longford and, I remember, he asked what would I do if he left Offaly? And I said it's a very easy answer, 'I'd go straight to the hurlers and I wouldn't play football again'.

It didn't happen like that. In 1983, I tore the ligaments off my left ankle, and I had to get a screw put in. And in 1984 then, in May, I was down in Shannonbridge power station and I was playing an inter-firms match against Galway in Padraig Pearses outside Ballinasloe.

I tore the ACL in my right knee... and that was more or less the end of my career. We couldn't get anyone to fix it. McGee found a guy in Dublin after about six months to do it and I got it done after that, but he didn't know I was a county hurler or footballer, and it broke down after the first match back in the National League down in Cork.

I went back to him again and I mentioned it to him. He said that if he knew I was a county player, he would have done it a different way. But it was too late!

He repaired it again, and I had to go back through the whole thing. I have a massive scar on my right knee and it still hurts when I kneel down.

I went to New York then, in 1989. My wife was teaching over there, but I couldn't get any work. I met Frankie Dwyer in the pub one night – the president of Leitrim GAA. He knew me and told me he would get me a job if I played for Leitrim over there. So, the first match anyway in Gaelic Park, I tore the ACL in my left knee.

The operation over there was class. I only have a three-inch scar and it is as good as ever, no pain in it... nothing. My confidence was never the same after I did mine, however, because I depended an awful lot on my speed, especially playing football. I was quick off the mark, and I couldn't trust the knee, even though it was sound.

I was mentally uncertain, and I couldn't trust it. That was the end of me really.

It was a short career but a good one.

I got to meet a man called Frank Burke.

Frank Burke fought in the GPO during the 1916 rising; he was 17 years of age. He was going to the school in St Enda's that Padraig Pearse started up; the Irish school in Rathfarnham.

He was arrested, sent to prison, interned and all that, and he got back to Ireland. He won All-Ireland hurling and football medals with Dublin... three All-Ireland football titles and two All-Ireland hurling titles, so there are only three people in the GAA who have All-Ireland hurling medals and football medals in successive years.

Frank Burke in the 20s and Jack Lynch in the 40s... and I achieved it in the 80s. I got honoured with a presentation in 1982 to recognise that feat. Jack Lynch was at the function in The Gresham Hotel, and my mother and father, brothers and sisters were all there.

Lynch spoke up and he said there's another man in this 'group 'and he is still alive and he lives very close to where I live. So, Eugene McGee organised to get a taxi. We left the function and went out to Rathfarnham, to Frank Burke's house.

He was 86 years of age at that time. And Jack Lynch and myself walked in, with Eugene McGee and an *Irish Press* photographer.

We met the man, and we were talking to him. Of course, it went over my head. I was too young to realise the importance of it all. He won All-Irelands and another claim to fame Frank Burke has, he was marking Mick Hogan in Croke Park when the Black and Tans came and Mick Hogan was shot.

Frank Burke was crawling off the pitch, the two of them and Hogan shouted out, 'I'm hit, I'm hit', and he died there on the pitch. Frank Burke was there beside him.

I was in the man's house, I shook his hand, and I have photographs. There are photographs in Eugene McGee's book too. I tell the story because I met and shook hands with a man that was associated with such history. It was *serious.* My father was there, and he used to smoke a pipe and the pipe was shaking in his mouth with excitement when he met Jack Lynch.

It was a special time.

”

MARK CORRIGAN

Mark Corrigan beats Dermot McCurtain to the ball in the All-Ireland final against Cork in Semple Stadium in 1984.

"

I PLAYED MY first senior game for Offaly against Tipperary in the league in 1979. We then got into an All-Ireland final with the Regional College in Athlone, but Offaly were due to play Waterford in the league the following day. Back then, you had to do well in the league to keep the county afloat.

It was nearly more important than the championship.

I got a massive buzz out of playing with the lads in Athlone, but I was told not to play with the college. The final was Saturday, and the game against Waterford was on the Sunday.

The manager in Athlone was in a bit of a state anyway, because he had been asked not to play me. I told him I didn't mind... I wanted to play. We went to the final anyway, and I was on the sideline.

It was on about 10 minutes and we were down five points... things were not looking good. I said that to them, and they asked me would I mind going in? I said, 'I don't!' The other lads were after putting in some shift to get us this far; it meant a lot to them.

In I went, and we won it. I went on the next day to the Waterford game, was thrown the No 12 jersey and we beat Waterford. There was nothing mentioned about it after.

We won a first ever under-21 Leinster then with Offaly. A lot of those players came into the senior panel and it made training very competitive.

In 1980, we won our first Leinster title and it never really sunk in with me at the time, what it meant to the older lads that were there... the likes of Damien Martin and Johnny Flaherty, who would have been there since '69. That was a great breakthrough, and some fantastic hurling was played. So, we won an under-21 and senior Leinster in a short space of time. It was a big high.

The 1981 All-Ireland was another first. It brought great enjoyment to people in Offaly and, suddenly, everything else didn't matter.

The first All-Ireland was very special.

I was only 16 when my father passed away. He hurled for Offaly back in 1929 and won a junior All Ireland playing in goals for them. Pat Carroll's father would have been in goals for Offaly as well in 1930.

My first thoughts after the final whistle were, if he was alive to see it, *My father would have enjoyed that.*

I thought we had a better team in 1982. That was *our* team and I feel we could have won the All-Ireland in 1982 and '83. The monkey was off our back, but Kilkenny beat us in the Leinster final.

We had a nice blend of youth and experience. We were all very loyal to each other. Club hurling was strong, but the county players backed each other up on the field of play. We valued each other.

Definitely, 1981 brought the whole county alive.

We were training out the back of the County Arms Hotel, and then you had the School teams training afterwards. It really lifted everyone.

There was a big lead up to it, too.

I worked for Loughnane Building Contractors at the time. Seamus Loughnane approached me to see if I wanted a few weeks off work before the final? I told him I didn't, because working was the best preparation for me. I was keeping busy and working away. He went off laughing at the time, thinking I would be mad for a bit of time off.

That was my make up. I wouldn't have been one for changing routines. I played in 11 Leinster finals and won seven of them, but I would have been in work the next morning after them all, the same as if nothing happened.

There was one particular time where I used to train at lunchtime. Willie Loughnane used to say to me, 'Some lads eat their dinner at lunchtime... but you train!'

I travelled to all the matches with Ger Coughlan; I never went on the bus. We had a routine. We would go to mass first, and then get a good steak breakfast into us. We would head to a field up in Dublin, usually in Crumlin... and puck around a few balls.

We would chat about the match... Ger was wing back and I was wing forward, so we would talk about different scenarios, things like signals for line-balls. Ger was a fantastic player. He had it all... guts, determination, vision and he never gave up. He was a terrier.

We would time it as such that we would arrive at the hotel at the same time as the rest of the lads on the bus. We were never too long in the one spot, and that was a routine throughout my career.

It was fantastic preparation to just leave your own parish and sail off at our own pace, chatting about the match the whole way up.

Before we went out onto the field, Diarmuid Healy pulled the half-forward line together and his instruction to us was that he wasn't worried about us not scoring... but the one thing he wanted us to do was stop the Galway half-back line from dominating. He told us that they were the strong point of their team, and he told us if we dominated them and kept the ball moving, we would win the All-Ireland.

Now, I was all about scoring, so for me to be listening to this... I didn't understand it at the time but, looking back on it, it was a very smart and well thought out move. It didn't make sense to me but, Healy had it perfectly read.

It was the key to our success. Brendan Bermingham pulled and broke more hurls, he definitely kept it moving.

They were a very good half-back line – Sylvie Linnane, Sean Silke and Iggy Clarke, and they won a lot of games from there when you look back on it because of the quality of ball they were putting into their forwards.

Also, Healy's timing in saying that to us was crucial. If he had said it to us in training, it would have been gone out the door. Diarmuid Healy was extremely cool under pressure and very good at reading games.

It was very tough hurling right through. We hurled very well.

We might not have been ready for it in 1980, though we were only pipped by a Bernie Forde goal. If it hadn't been for that, we would have been right there.

There was nothing between us and Galway, and it was always some hurling.

I was right beside Johnny Flaherty for the goal at the end.

When Bermingham took the pass off Delaney, I started to move in. I thought Johnny was going to pass it to me… there were two lads around him.

Johnny was very strong but you kind of thought, *This attack is going nowhere.*

But then he hand-passed the ball into the net. Johnny was phenomenal and probably the best forward I have seen. Offaly didn't see enough of him. He was 10 or 12 years in America. Even in club hurling, when he came home he was super.

At the final whistle, everything just erupted.

There were Offaly people everywhere and a tremendous buzz. We got the train back to Tullamore the next day and there were flares being let off.

We had a great set-up, to be fair. It was great for the management team to get there in the end. They pulled us together as a unit and that was the real key to the success.

Diarmuid Healy brought in a belief that, *It's not over, until it's over.* When you look back on the likes of Kilkenny… how many games have they won with a late score or in extra time? That is the way they played.

He brought that into us. Anything can happen in 70 minutes.

We adopted that approach and stayed hurling until the bitter end. Things looked bleak in many a game, but we always stayed plugging away and hung in.

It created *something* back in the clubs as well. It raised the standard and things got going at the grassroots. The grassroots are the key because, if you don't have it there, you won't have it at the top.

It was brilliant to see all the minor success in the 1980s as well. I'm sure by us winning the All Irelands, it gave them a great lift. They would have been thinking that they could do this too.

Brother Vincent and Brother Denis did great work in Birr, but there were also great men in all the different parishes. In Kinnitty, you had Fr Madden and the school principal Michael Dooley. They created teams there and their passion for it was brilliant.

Kinnitty were strong at the time too. You had the likes of Johnny Flaherty, Pat Delaney, Mick Cleere… a tremendous club team.

I remember, when I was young, asking Will Cordial, 'What do I have to do to make it?'

He had a walking stick with a knob on the top of it, and would be spinning it around in his hand. He told me if I could do that with the hurl, that I would be grand.

I told him I would practice that, but he told me that he wasn't finished and he asked, 'Have you a skipping rope?' I didn't!

'You start skipping and then start to dance, and move from side to side!' he said. His thinking was that if I got my wrists and side-step right, I would make it and he was bang on the money.

Tommy Fogarty and Jackie Ryland in Banagher… every club had their own superstars that worked tirelessly for the GAA.

I captained Offaly in 1989 and we won the Leinster title.

That was special too, because in 1889 my grandfather had captained Cadamstown to win a county title and, one hundred years on… here was I bringing back the Bob O'Keefe Cup to Kinnitty. I scored 3-7 in the Leinster final… very satisfying day all round!

I put a lot into it and prepared myself well. The only thing that mattered to me was to win. If that didn't happen, I would always go back and analyse why we didn't win and if there was something different we could have done.

Especially as a forward, our aim was to put the scores on the scoreboard. It's no good if you don't get the scores.

I really enjoyed the journey with the camogie team as well, that started in 2008.

A couple of years previously, I was asked to go in with them, but I didn't. I was always thinking that they had such great players, such as Michaela Morkan, Elaine Dermody, Marion Crean and Sheila Sullivan... it would have been terrible to see them go through their career with no medal.

I had my own daughter Aoife, and she was starting to come on to it. When Joachim Kelly asked me to get involved, I didn't even have to think about it. The first year we were beaten in the All-Ireland final and then we went on to win two All Irelands in-a-row... the junior in 2009 and the intermediate in 2010.

They weren't too far off winning a senior All-Ireland either; we were pushing the likes of Kilkenny and the big teams at this stage. Yet we fell back... and they went on to win All-Irelands. They had the players, but you can't stay going forever, I suppose.

I enjoyed my time with Ollie Baker as a selector with the senior hurlers as well. We probably got the team a bit too late. A few of them were coming to the end and we had to ask them to give us another few years. When we didn't win it was a downer, but I think we improved things when we were in there.

I won seven Leinster titles and one stat I have is that I was never on an Offaly team that was beaten in the first round of the championship. They were great days, and every time I see the Offaly jersey now I get this shot of adrenaline... it doesn't matter who is wearing it.

JIM TROY

OFFALY 3-18 KILKENNY 3-18
Leinster SHC Semi-Final
Croke Park
JUNE 23, 1985

Jim Troy waves to the crowd after being honoured as a member of the 1985 Offaly Jubilee team during the All-Ireland Senior Championship final in 2010.

★ **OFFALY: J Troy**; L Carroll, E Coughlan, P Fleury; A Fogarty, P Delaney (0-4), G Coughlan; D Owens (0-1), J Kelly (1-1); P Corrigan (1-6), M Coughlan, P Carroll (0-1); M Corrigan (1-2), P Horan (0-2), J Dooley (0-1). Subs: T Conneely for L Carroll, D Fogarty for M Coughlan.

★ **KILKENNY:** D Burke; J Henderson, P Brennan, J Marnell; J Hennessy, G Henderson, P Prendergast; G Fennelly (0-3), R Heffernan (0-1); P Walsh (0-3), R Power (0-2), K Brennan (0-4); H Ryan (0-5), C Heffernan (1-0), L Fennelly (2-0). Subs: J Murphy for R Heffernan, B Fitzpatrick for Murphy.

THE ACTION

OFFALY PRODUCED AN unbelievable fightback, coming from nine points down at one stage in the second-half to reel Kilkenny in and force a replay for the right to advance to the Leinster senior hurling final.

Kilkenny ruled the roost for three quarters of the contest as a misfiring Offaly struggled to come to terms with the game. With Pat Delaney a collosus at centre-back, Offaly turned the screw in the last quarter and lived to fight another day.

Kilkenny stormed into the game, and Offaly needed a Mark Corrigan goal on 15 minutes to help find their feet. They then went ahead through the impressive Danny Owens, before Liam Fennelly fired his second goal past a helpless Jim Troy from the penalty spot. At half-time, the Cats led by 2-9 to 1-8 with Offaly lucky to be so close.

Within 35 seconds of the restart, Christy Heffernan got the Cats' third goal, while a brace of points followed and Offaly were in serious trouble. Mark and Paddy Corrigan were doing their best to stem the tide with scores, but a nine point lead opened up.

Then, within seven minutes, the lead was cut to two points. Joachim Kelly pointed before a fortunate Paddy Corrigan free from 50 metres found its way to the net. Joe Dooley, and another long range free from Delaney, brought it back to 3-13 to 2-14.

Fifteen minutes from time, Offaly were level when Joachim Kelly flicked a Delaney free to the net, before Padraig Horan amazingly put them into the lead.

Offaly went two up but Kilkenny replied to set up a mouth-watering final 10 minutes. Kilkenny led coming into the closing stages, but Paddy Corrigan proved the Offaly chief rescue officer with a free to force a replay.

★★★★★

"

AFTER WE WERE beaten in the 1984 All-Ireland final we came back to Birr and we said, 'Oh, we'll win the All-Ireland next year!'... all of these promises were made.

I had played in 1982 in a couple of matches, and I was actually dropped for a couple of matches in the summer in '83. I was under pressure starting off. Those couple of matches in 1982 didn't work out, and Damien Martin got back.

So, it was either make or break... I was 25 at this stage.

Kilkenny are always hard beaten, but they would have been favourites going into 1985. It was a bad time for us, after losing the All-Ireland. People were on about how good Cork were in 1984, and everything. But there weren't too many changes to our team.

After promising the people that we'd win the All-Ireland in 1985, it would have been very damaging for Offaly hurling to go out in the first game in the championship.

It was still the same full-back line from the year before. We got off to a bad start in that Leinster semi-final, but we were only four points down at half-time with Kilkenny after doing all the hurling. They should have got more scores... they had a lot of wides.

When we got back out after half-time, Christy Heffernan got a goal. The ball had hardly been thrown in, I'd say.

We kept plugging away, anyway... Paddy Corrigan's frees kept us in it. They put Joachim in centre-forward and brought Pat Carroll, God rest him, out to centrefield. Danny Owens hurled well. Tom Conneely came on and hurled very well that day too at wing back, and Aidan Fogarty was dropped back to corner-back.

Liam Fennelly was going to town at corner-forward, so we put Fogarty back on him and we got a goal... Paddy Corrigan, a free... a kind of a lucky goal. Then, we got a long range free! Pat Delaney took it and Joachim was in... it could have been near the full-forward line at this stage, and Joachim swung with one hand and buried it to the back of the net.

We went ahead after that, but Kilkenny came back and they went two points ahead again. Paddy Corrigan got a point to equalise it, and that was it.

They got three goals. One of them... Fennelly hit it and I couldn't have stopped it, it was right up in the corner. And Christy Heffernan hand-passed one to the net. I can't remember the other goal. I didn't do too bad... puck-outs were good, but it was a kind of make or break for me that day.

I was under pressure but, in fairness to Diarmuid Healy, he came to me and said, 'We need you now!' Damien Martin was pushing on at this stage and he wasn't going to last forever. Healy told me, 'You'll be the goalie now!' He did an awful lot of work with me.

At the time, I think I even lost two stone in 1985.

He did an awful lot of work with me and some of the stuff he did with me, you'd kind of laugh at... more mentality stuff. He would have you relaxing, letting yourself go down... flat out on the ground... and you'd have lads laughing at us. The likes of Pat Carroll laughing at us... but Pat was a great man!

I had a better game in the replay. Once I got over that drawn game – and that was the one to get over – I was picked the next day. I saved two penalties in the replay.

I wouldn't be one hundred percent sure but, at the time, the talk was that Kilkenny had never been beaten in a replay in Leinster. We beat them by six points in the replay!

I can't remember how good that match was, but I know the first penalty... it was Adrian Ronan who took it and I got a block. The second one was Ray Heffernan, a brother of Christy's... and I saved it as well.

Damien Martin had been there since 1969. It was unbelievable.

Even in 1982, when we played Wexford, Damien was at the back of the goals carrying hurls. RTE made a big thing out of that, but he wasn't doing anything to me... he didn't disrupt my game or anything.

I would have known him all my life. He lives out the Lusmagh Road in Banagher and we'd always see him going in and out. Sure he used to cut turf in Lusmagh.

He was a good mentor. Even in the dressing-room, he would always have something positive to say. When we won the All-Ireland that year in 1985, he was probably the first man on the field to me from the dug-out.

He often said afterwards that we'd never have won the All Ireland if it wasn't for me in the replay with Kilkenny... but I thought he was only being nice to me.

I think I put in a good effort from the time they dropped me in 1983. I had lost a bit of weigh. Diarmuid Healy had kept on to me... and on to me, but he eventually got me to lose it.

I think Padraig Horan said at the homecoming in 1981 that the only thing Diarmuid Healy failed to do was to knock two stone off Jim Troy!

He nearly had us brainwashed going out in the 1985 All-Ireland, that if we didn't win this... there were farmers in Offaly who were in terrible situations, under awful stress... and things could get worse. He said that if we won the All Ireland we could save their lives.

I remember Pat Fleury in the 1985 All Ireland final.

At that time, everything was done to a time-plan. Offaly were 'out' at two minutes to three or whatever time it was... you had a time, you got your slot to leave the dressing-room. So, when Healy was talking in the dressing-room, you would hear a pin drop.

You'd hear everything he was saying. We got to the door, anyway... and, of course, the head steward wouldn't let us out.

Fleury hit the door a belt and your man closed the door... locked us in, I think. That was grand anyway, and maybe two minutes after... knock on the door. The steward stuck his head in the door.

I never heard Healy getting cross before... cursing.

He let a roar out at your man and said, 'WE'LL F***ING GO OUT WHEN WE ARE F***ING READY!'

He'd have us riled up to the last!

You would be under terrible pressure before an All-Ireland final. You'd be worrying, whereas when I got out, I'd be okay on the field. Your stomach would be churning and for a whole week before it, you'd have nightmares that you're going to let a ball fall out of your hand and into the net.

You don't enjoy an All-Ireland final... not until it's over. And the thing about a goalkeeper is... one slip up, and you're... GONE!

After losing the 1986 Leinster final, Healy came in after the match – the minors were after winning the Leinster final before it – and he said, 'Lads, if it's any consolation to you, we won the right Leinster final today'.

He continued, 'Only for you lads, they would never have won it today'. We were after losing our Leinster final, and he still made us feel kind of good about ourselves.

And I think, in hindsight, he was right. It was important to win that minor because probably one of the best teams that Offaly ever had came out of those minors. In the 90s, when they came on, their skill and everything was unbelievable.

In Lusmagh, hurling was everything. We played junior C football, but that would never worry you until the morning of the match.

My brother John and myself went to the field in Lusmagh pitch before one of the All-Irelands. Next thing, there were people with cameras... and children getting photographs. Listen, they didn't knock us off or anything but you couldn't get away from it.

The Offaly county team was nearly like a club team really, because it was such a small knit area. I'd say there are lads in Kilkenny and Cork, and wherever, that wouldn't know anything about the other players, whereas we knew each other's brothers and sisters, fathers and mothers.

We knew what land they had... and what they had at home in the yard.

Diarmuid Healy never had you lose focus, and he was right. We played Laois in the Leinster final in 1985 and one of the things he said to us was, 'Laois have run ye close in several matches, but they've never played ye in a Leinster final'.

They had never hurled in a Leinster final, but we had. I actually hadn't... but Offaly had.

The relief when it's all over, you can go out and enjoy yourself for a few days, have a few pints... and it was great to go around and meet people. You'd have a week's holidays booked in.

Winning an All-Ireland with John in 1994 was one of the highlights but, unfortunately, my father didn't live to see that... he was a mighty hurling man. My mother was there, and she didn't miss any of the matches.

I was 34 at this stage.

The 1994 team was a very skilful team and when you look at it, with five minutes to go, I thought to myself, *This is all over.* When Gary Kirby got a free to make it five points, you couldn't see Offaly winning it, in fairness.

Eamonn Cregan was a good manager. He was along the same lines as Healy but he wasn't as diplomatic. He was more of a shouting man and beating the hurl against the ground, but Healy was different... soft spoken, getting into your head. But both men had the same ideas about hurling.

Derry O'Donovan was the physical trainer. Derry told us before the 1994 All Ireland, 'These lads are going to be fit, but Offaly are the best hurlers'. In fairness to Johnny Dooley going for goal... Limerick probably thought he was going to tap it over the bar.

I played with some great players in my day, especially lads in the full-back line. You always have to have a good understanding with your full-back especially, because he's the man directly in front of you.

Eugene Coughlan especially, you'd have to shout 'MY Ball' or whatever. And then, after you had let out the shout, you'd have to make sure nobody got a touch on it... or a tip of a hurl.

Tom Dempsey from Wexford said one time, 'You'll hear Troy roaring wide ball'.

”

PADRAIG HORAN

OFFALY 2-11 GALWAY 1-12
All-Ireland SHC Final
Croke Park
SEPTEMBER 1, 1985

Padraig Horan and Joachim Kelly celebrate together on the steps of the Hogan Stand after Offaly defeated Galway in the 1985 All-Ireland final.

★ **OFFALY:** J Troy; A Fogarty, E Coughlan, P Fleury; T Conneely, P Delaney, G Coughlan; J Kelly, D Owens; P Corrigan (0-5), B Bermingham (0-1), M Corrigan (0-2); P Cleary (2-0), **P Horan (0-3)**, J Dooley. Subs: D Fogarty for Owens, B Keeshan for Conneely.

★ **GALWAY:** P Murphy; O Kilkenny, C Hayes, S Linnane; P Finnerty, T Keady (0-1), T Kilkenny; M Connolly, S Mahon; M McGrath (0-1), B Lynskey (0-2), J Cooney (0-1); B Forde, N Lane (0-1), PJ Molloy (1-6). Subs: J Murphy for McGrath, A Cunningham for Forde, M Haverty for Connolly.

THE ACTION

OFFALY CLAIMED THEIR second All-Ireland senior hurling title in five years by edging out Galway in a tough and physical encounter. Having fallen to Cork in the 1984 decider, the team bounced back and, while they rode their luck at times, they hung in and sealed the deal.

It was a day when their patience and experience came to the fore. Galway struck 19 wides over the course of the game, including a massive 14 in the opening half, while Offaly proved more efficient with just eight wides over the 70 minutes. Two Pat Cleary goals were crucial on the day, with his first putting Offaly into the lead on 28 minutes, before another goal just 30 seconds into the second-half left five in it.

Galway had the better of the opening exchanges, even if they were finding scores hard to come by. With both defences on top, the action was tight but, after Noel Lane and Paddy Corrigan exchanged points, Cleary struck for his first goal after he capitalised on Peter Murphy blocking down a Paddy Corrigan free.

Noel Lane and PJ Molloy were carrying the Galway charge, but with Corrigan nailing the frees and Padraig Horan also finding his range, Offaly went in leading 1-6 to 0-7 at half-time. A mere 30 seconds after the restart Cleary grabbed his second goal. Points from Brendan Bermingham and Mark Corrigan put Offaly seven points in front, and it looked like they would kick for home.

Molloy and Galway had other ideas, however, and by the 45th minute Molloy had hit 1-3 in reply, with his goal coming after he caught a high ball and finished to the net. With only a point in the game, Offaly had to show some bottle and they had plenty of it. Jim Troy made an heroic double save from Molloy, and then from Noel Lane, to slow down the Galway march, while two Paddy Corrigan frees tamed the Galway tide.

Padraig Horan swung over his third point of the game for an inspirational score four minutes from time and, while Galway did get another one from a Tony Keady '65', it was Pat Fleury who had the honour of receiving the Liam MacCarthy Cup.

★★★★★

"

IT ALL STARTED for me in 1966. I got a call on a Saturday evening to say I was to be in Mullingar on the Sunday to play minor hurling with Offaly. I was only 16. I remember the weather was brutal and the senior game was called off because the pitch was unplayable, but they played the minor.

I had a particularly good game, my first time in an Offaly jersey. When the game was over, Paddy Molloy came over to me and shook my hand. That was great because Paddy was a folk hero at the time. He was probably 'the man' back then and now as well. He was a great hurler.

And then, I came on to the Offaly seniors at 19 years of age. We played Waterford in Waterford, and I remember Paddy Spellman came over and shook my hand before the game, wishing me the best of luck. Paddy was another former great hurler. That's how it started.

I was there until 1987.

Everyone knows the team of the 80s and everyone knows the team of the 90s but no one remembers the team of the 70s.... and there were a lot of good hurlers at that time who got nowhere.

Talking about lads outside of the hurling area, that time we had Frank Monaghan and Pat Corcoran from Rahan, two good lads. Eugene Hannon was an outstanding full-back. Terry Leonard... he went to Australia, and there was Ger Milne and John Ryan... both had bad accidents, two fine midfielders from Birr.

They never won anything... Joe Hernon never won anything, Joe Dooley of St Rynagh's never won anything. They were all really good hurlers, but people don't talk about them.

Those teams in the 70s were very good. I remember playing Galway in Galway and they had a flyer of a wing forward. I was playing centre-back that time. The flyer from Galway, I think Barrett was his name, was coming down the line and I went out and met him, and landed him on the ground. I turned around, and the referee Sean O'Meara was laughing.

We beat Galway that day, and again, they were just another team at that time as far as we were concerned. We had no fear. So hurling didn't begin in the 80s... it began way before that.

I feel sorry when I hear people talking about hurling and not mentioning some of those hurlers that I recalled, because they were great bits of stuff. Dominic Kelly from Killeigh wasn't from the hurling area, but he was very good.

Even Mick O'Rourke from Killeigh. Mick was playing one day... we were playing Waterford and Mick was playing wing back. I was centre back. Waterford were fierce dirty on the day and we were running out of subs. I turned around to O'Rourke and said, 'It's about time we were levelling things up here now'.

The ball came in anyway and, as I'm up catching, O'Rourke pulled and made s***e out of my hand. I turned around to him and said, 'I meant Waterford players!'

You would think Offaly hurling was only invented in 1981 the way some people go on. We were almost there. If we had better coaching and more organisation, we might have won something earlier.

Brother Denis brought a bit of shape to the thing in the 60s and 70s, and then Andy Gallagher took up the reins for a while, before Diarmuid Healy came on board and those three men made huge changes in hurling in Offaly.

There was no unity before that. Lads would go into the dressing-room, and we'd sit in the one corner and, for example, the Drumcullen lads would sit in the other corner. The management started introducing more social activities, meeting after games and having a cup of tea... and playing cards.

That broke down the barriers and brought it all together.

We had no issue with playing Galway; we took them on several times and beat them.

That's why I couldn't understand 1981. When we beat Galway in the All-Ireland, their noses were out of joint. They felt they were so much superior to us and they made that known, yet they couldn't beat us.

In particular, I think the 1985 All-Ireland for me was great. I played in 1981 when I had a groin strain, but I wasn't going to miss out on an All- Ireland final, even if I had to be carried out. Then, in 1984, Cork beat us in Thurles – and some players from other counties said the game was better off with a traditional county in an All-Ireland final, rather than Offaly.

So, 1985 for me, was the greatest satisfaction of the lot. We came back to win it, and proved them all wrong.

At that time as well, we did things that were stupid. We thought they were great, but they were stupid. I spent more time fighting lads than hurling – I changed all that in the later years, and I found everything a lot easier and a lot more enjoyable.

Attitudes changed, and there was more emphasis on hurling and using our skills rather than our physique.

The 1985 All-Ireland was typical Galway, they had all the possession. Diarmuid Healy had us from 1980 on and always said to us, 'If you're close to Galway, you'll beat them... because they will fall apart'. I remember that was a Kilkenny attitude too.

When I was hurling full-back with Leinster back in the early 70s, I was the only Offaly man on it and they said the same thing to me when we were playing Connacht. 'If you're close to Galway, don't worry about them... you'll beat them.' That was a Kilkenny thing alright, and it was something that Healy carried into Offaly.

I always loved playing centre-forward.

I remember Paudie Delaney suggesting to bring me to centre-forward... and I went out to centre-forward in the 1985 All-Ireland final. It was one of the best games I ever had, even though I was 35 years of age.

I had started playing centre forward with the club, and I was more use there than full-forward. I was moved out during the game in 1985. We talked about it in training. We should have done it in 1984, but we didn't. Of course, in 1985 as well, a lot of people did it for Pat Carroll. Pat was a brilliant county man; he was all for the team and he never put himself first... that All-Ireland was for him.

I remember the national anthem well. Galway had a Murphy chap in goals and he was fierce nervous, and we knew he was nervous. So, when the anthem was being played, I went and stood in behind him and kept pushing up against him.

He f***ed me out of it when I met him afterwards. He was nervous, and he had this 'thug' going in behind him, pushing him... digging him and prodding him.

I also remember Pat Cleary's goal... the rebound. Two of us connected on the ball together. Sylvie Linnane had been jeering us before that about not scoring goals, so we gave him a fierce going over with that, the poor lad.

Another ball broke, as I was out centre-forward.

I came flying onto it and there was no one inside on Pat Cleary. I pulled on it, and it hit off Sylvie's shin and went back out. If Cleary got in, we'd have had a third goal only for that.

In 1980, we won the Leinster Championship, and my father died during the game. I did an interview with Mícheál Ó Muircheartaigh, and he knew what had happened… someone else had told him. Then they told me after. That was tough, and not only for me, but for all the lads as well.

They were in Banagher the following evening at my father's funeral instead of celebrating.

In general, as a team, we pulled well together. I was in the forwards. I probably would have preferred to be in the backs, but Healy asked me to go up into the forwards. I spent a lot of time knocking lads down and making room for Mark Corrigan and Johnny Flaherty and them. We all had to play our bit, but I'd have preferred a different role.

It was for the team… and that was it.

We were involved in some rough tussles as well in those early years. I remember down in Tulla in the late 70s, it was the making of us. We played Clare and a row broke out after the game… Pat Carroll got hit and a ferocious row broke out. I wasn't involved in the row, for once. I was down the other end of the field.

I was with Noel O'Donoghue, the referee, coming off the field and I looked up and saw the row going on. I headed for the gate and, next thing, a Clare crowd came charging towards me.

There was an auld fella with an umbrella coming first and I pulled, and I hit him on the forehead. Who arrived beside me… only Willie Gorman. A couple of cousins got in beside me, and I got in as far as the dressing-room. We were locked in the dressing-room for an hour… couldn't get out.

We were banned from playing matches at home, and so were Clare. We had to play all of our matches away, and that made us. It made us because we always had the idea that we would beat anyone in Birr but, now, we had to hurl outside of Birr… and it made the Offaly team.

We started travelling together to matches, closer together. We started having more training sessions with hurling in them and we learned to concentrate more on the ball, rather than on the man.

Another day was a great day for Offaly hurling.

I wasn't playing, I was injured at the time, when Offaly played Cork in a relegation battle in Thurles. I remember Joe Mooney was hurling at the time, another man that never won anything either… a good hurler from Clareen. They beat Cork. That was a huge day for Offaly because Cork had to win the game… and they weren't able to win it.

I think we were also lucky with the people we had over us. And one man who never got credit, but he was excellent at that time, was Tony Murphy. No matter how serious things were, Tony always saw the funny side of it. Some of the situations were very tense and Tony would lighten the whole tone with some craic or some remark.

One regret I have is never winning an All-Ireland Club Championship. We were beaten in four finals – three, and a replay. I felt we were good enough to do it, but we didn't do it, especially against Loughgiel Shamrocks from Antrim. We drew with them in Croke Park and went and played the replay in Belfast.

We shouldn't have done it. It was madness of the highest order.

Another great win which I look back on was Birr Community School in an All-Ireland 'A' colleges. I was manager of the school team along with Jimmy Dunne and Frank Bergin. We had Gary Cahill, Daithí Regan and all of those lads on it. That was a fierce achievement for a community school for a start, a mixed school.

Up to then, it was all boarding schools winning it out… and they were bringing in lads from all over the place to hurl with them. We had a great bunch of lads who all went on to win minor All-Irelands and senior All-Irelands.

Birr coming and winning an All-Ireland… that was terrific altogether. Even though it was Birr, and I was St Rynagh's, I had taught nearly all of the Birr lads. The connection was there, as I had them from first year up.

The first one they won, it was a stormy day in Croke Park. We drew with Dunloy, and beat them in the replay.

I made great friends out of it from every county. Actually, I will always give credit to Cork because whenever we went down to Cork, they looked after us really well. They would bring us down to St Finbarr's before the match and they were brilliant to us!

In the 80s we had great players, but only the bare 15, 16… 17 lads. At that time, there was no such thing as a panel of 30. But we had outstanding players.

The great thing about it at the time was if, say Kinnitty felt they had a good wing back, they could talk to Diarmuid Healy and ask to bring him in and try him out. There was no such thing as saying, 'That f***er is from Kinnitty, leave him where he is!'

He would bring him and try him out.

It didn't matter where you were from, that became the main thing and the team got close. My best friend was probably Pat Fleury. There was a time Drumcullen and Rynagh's would have been big rivals. But, to this day, Pat is still my best friend, along with Joachim Kelly and Brendan Bermingham.

PAT JOE WHELAHAN

OFFALY 3-15 KILKENNY 4-9
Leinster SHC Final
Croke Park
JULY 9, 1989

His days winning and losing, but mostly winning with so many club and county teams has left Pat Joe Whelahan with so many memories, but here he is with Birr during the All-Ireland club final in 2003.

★ **OFFALY:** J Troy; A Fogarty, E Coughlan, M Hanamy; R Mannion, P Delaney, G Coughlan; J Kelly (0-1), J Pilkington (0-1); M Duignan, D Regan, M Corrigan (3-7); D Pilkington (0-1), V Teehan (0-1), D Owens. Subs: J Dooley (0-3) for Regan, P Corrigan (0-1) for Owens.

★ **KILKENNY:** K Fennelly; J Henderson, P Dwyer, W O'Connor; J Power, M Cleere (0-1), S Fennelly; G Fennelly, L Egan; A Prendergast, R Power (0-2), M Phelan; A Ronan (0-5), C Heffernan (1-0), L Fennelly (2-0). Subs: B Hennessy for J Power, L McCarthy (1-1) for Phelan.

THE ACTION

OFFALY EXPERIENCED SOME nervy moments late on, but in the end had three points to spare over Kilkenny as Mark Corrigan lifted the Bob O'Keefe Cup for the Faithful County.

Offaly were coasting to their win with 12 minutes to play, leading 3-13 to 1-7, before an almighty Kilkenny comeback saw them grab three goals.

Jim Troy and the full-back line of Aidan Fogarty, Eugene Coughlan and Martin Hanamy were teak tough, while Ger Coughlan, Joachim Kelly, Joe Dooley and Michael Duignan all contributed handsomely but it was captain Mark Corrigan who led by example, landing a personal tally of 3-7.

Offaly boss Pat Joe Whelahan sprung Joe Dooley from the bench just before half-time, and he made his mark landing three points from play which, in the end, proved vital. That opening half never really sprung to life, but Corrigan fired home the first of his three goals just before half-time to send Offaly in, leading 1-7 to 1-3.

After an even start to the second-half, Offaly began to move through the gears. Michael Duignan was causing problems for the Kilkenny defence and he laid on two more goals for Corrigan to send Offaly cruising. Throw in a penalty save from Jim Troy, after he denied Adrian Ronan, and it looked like Whelahan's men would do a right number on the Cats.

Kilkenny had other ideas and, with a blitz of their own, hit three goals from Christy Heffernan, Liam McCarthy and a second for Liam Fennelly to cut the Offaly lead to two. With the game in the melting pot and the momentum with Kilkenny, Corrigan stepped up to break the cycle and land a point to see Offaly through to an All-Ireland semi-final clash with Antrim.

★★★★★

"

I HAVE BEEN involved in so much. Between clubs in Offaly, clubs in other counties... minor teams and senior teams, I don't know where to start. I am 76 now and, over my life, I have worked with so many top-class hurlers from so many different counties.

Vincent Hogan of the *Irish Independent* is a very good friend of mine and I would have done a lot of interviews with him over the years. I would love to sit down with someone and go through it all. I have made so many friends through hurling. Only a couple of weeks ago, Cork were playing Offaly in Birr... and Dr Con Murphy came up to see me.

But 1989 was a special year in my life.

I trained the three Offaly teams – the minors, under-21's and the seniors. We won the three Leinster finals, and beat Kilkenny in all three of them.

That year, Diarmuid Healy was training Kilkenny and I was training Offaly. We were due to play Kilkenny in a league game in Birr but whatever wrangling was done, they got the game moved to Tullamore. The line that came out was that the pitch in Birr was unplayable... but it was!

They beat us that day in Tullamore and I was raging over it. Anyway, it came to the Leinster final and we met again. We beat them in the final and I remember thinking to myself, *They can have those two league points, but we have the Leinster cup.*

We were 11 points up in that senior final with about nine minutes to go. I was walking around by the Cusack Stand and we were flying it. Kilkenny got three goals and I looked up into the stand and just thought... *Please don't let this happen to me!*

The biggest disappointment that year was Antrim beating us in the All-Ireland senior semi-final. I really wanted to get to an All-Ireland final and play Tipperary... it would have been great.

The night before that Antrim game, we had a meeting and a meal in Dooly's Hotel in Birr. We sat down and talked about a few things, but I remember going home and saying to Susan that I thought we were in trouble for the game the next day.

Things just didn't feel right and some of the players... their heads were wrong. Antrim were a good team, to be fair to them.

I went to Croke Park for the All-Ireland final and Antrim brought me into the dressing-room beforehand. The chairman asked me to come in and say a few words to them. They had this big long table in the middle of the dressing-room full of fruit. I never saw anything like it.

We gave them a Guard of Honour after they beat us, and that was a big thing. We were always known for our sportsmanship.

After that defeat, I was back training the minors on the Tuesday night. I was happy to get back at it straight away. We were six Sundays in-a-row in Croke Park that year. Every Sunday morning getting onto the bus... it was great.

We beat Clare in the All-Ireland minor final in 1989, but another one got away from us. We played Tipperary in the All-Ireland under-21 final that year too and we should have beaten them. There was a massive crowd at that game in Portlaoise. There was something like 10,000 people turned away. People broke the gates down and everything.

I remember walking across the field at one stage. Adrian Cahill and John Leahy were after getting into a row. Adrian was on the ground and, as I was walking over to check on him, the vibrations were coming out of the ground, such was the crowd there.

We went seven points up at one stage in the game. Tipperary were only after winning the senior All-Ireland.

I won three All-Ireland minor titles with the Offaly minors.

The first minor All-Ireland title in 1986 was huge. We beat Cork in the final. The following year we won it again, beating Tipperary.

I wasn't happy with the team we picked for the Leinster final against Kilkenny in 1987. Brian Whelahan and Johnny Dooley weren't on it... they were only young lads at 16.

We played Galway in a challenge match before the final. I left off a few of the starters as I wanted to get a look at some of the other players. Galway were 30 points up at half-time but by the finish, we got it down to about 14 points. I got what I wanted out of it and got to see what I wanted to see.

Galway then played Kilkenny in a challenge the following weekend and

Kilkenny beat them well. One of the Galway lads rang me the night before the Leinster final, and he asked me how we were fixed?

I told him we had a chance and to look out for 'one thing' in Croke Park tomorrow. I told him that we would not rise the ball... that we were going to keep everything on the ground. Kilkenny had no answer to us, and we beat them by seven points. Fan Larkin was over Kilkenny at the time.

We did the same against Tipperary in the All-Ireland final as well.

We played Kilkenny in the under-21 Leinster final in 1989. The likes of DJ Carey and Pat O'Neill were playing for Kilkenny... they had a great team. We beat them in Portlaoise. Johnny Dooley was only a sub; he had been sick so didn't start. I brought him on with about 20 minutes to go and he walked up and put a free straight over the bar with his first puck of the ball. A gifted hurler.

I don't know how I got the three jobs in 1989, but I do remember getting the minor job in 1986. Gerry Carroll from Shinrone was the minor chairman in Offaly at the time. There were four or five names in for the job, but I went for it anyway. I was driving over to Tullamore to meet them and I stopped the car in Kilcormac, and I said to myself... *I am wasting my time here, I'm not going to get the job!* I was going to turn around and go home but I kept going, and I ended up getting the job.

That year, I brought in six or seven really young lads on to the Offaly minor panel but they weren't on the team. I brought them in to train them up and we brought them everywhere with us. Then when 1987 came, they were ready! Kilkenny beat us in a Leinster minor final in 1988... DJ Carey was there that day.

Back then, it was 24 players on a minor panel. Galway would have had 50 players all vying for that last place on their panel, but we only had about 60 players in total to pick our panel from! That's how lopsided it is!

Those minor teams backboned some great senior teams after. We got 15 great years out of them.

The first club All-Ireland I won with Birr was in 1995 when we beat Sarsfields from Galway in the final.

Padraig Horan won the first club All-Ireland with Birr, but I was over the team for the second one in 1995. All my lads were playing which was something special. Barry and Simon were only around 19 and 20 at the time.

I remember one night in particular. We were training for one of the club All-Irelands. People came from all over to watch us. I loved to train the lads on a small hill. I was a big believer in sharp sprints because they are good for the legs. This long distance running is no good for your legs, if you are trying to cover 10 yards.

We trained so hard, that the lads would get the shakes from it.

I trained Toomevara and Nenagh to county titles in Tipperary as well. Nenagh have only won the one, which is mad given it's a big town. Another one that sticks out in my mind is Killimordaly in Galway... Tony Keady's club. I came in to train them and I made him captain. The poor man has passed away since.

I loved training teams and trained in loads of different counties, such as Laois, Galway and Tipperary – I was very popular in Tipperary. I won two county titles with Toomevara. I worked with some great men there, in particular the likes of Tommy Dunne and Roger Ryan.

When I was hurling myself, I won my first county final in 1965 with St Rynagh's and we went on to win five in-a-row. I hurled with them for over 20 years... and then I came into Birr.

I hurled with some great warriors with Offaly as well... Murphy, Flanagan and Spellman, all dead and gone since. Speedy Burke was a great friend of mine.

In 1969 we beat Wexford in the Leinster semi-final... they were All-Ireland champions. We hurled great that day. It took us about two days to come home from Croke Park. Myself, Barney Moylan, Paudge Mulhare and a few more went to the carnival in Cloghan on the way back from Dublin. They were great days.

We had great memories with the team of the late 60s and early 70s. We went down to hurl Waterford one year in a place up the mountains. I was down at one end of the field and when I looked down the other end of the field, I couldn't see the goals. The mist had come down half-way.

Austin Flynn played his last game for Waterford that day. A great player... he was one of the main men in Waterford hurling at the time.

You take the likes of Paddy Molloy and Barney Moylan; they never killed themselves training and would never do, say, six rounds of the field, but over 10 yards? They were brilliant. If a ball fell in front of us now... they would have it gone. They were gifted hurlers.

I had great years in St Rynagh's and Birr. You can't really compare the two. I won five Offaly senior hurling titles in-a-row with St Rynagh's as a player, and five in-a-row with Birr as manager.

I was very grateful to be honoured with the Offaly GAA Hall of Fame. I remember the night of the awards and the bit was being read out about my achievements... and Ollie Baker, the former Clare hurler, came down to me and asked how the hell I won all that?

I have a room in the house full of medals... Leinster and All-Irelands, you name it!

Offaly is a great county... just look at Shane Lowry. He came into our pub in Birr one Sunday, and we had a great day with him. He went in behind the bar and filled a pint with Brian. I really enjoyed the time in his company.

I walked in and I never copped him. Brian had to come out to me and tell me who I was after walking past. I had a great chat with him.

JOHNNY PILKINGTON

UCD 2-21 UCC 4-14
(after extra-time)
Fitzgibbon Cup Final
Waterford
MARCH 14, 1993

Johnny Pilkington (second from right on the back, with the Offaly team before the 1998 All-Ireland final) played with some amazing skilful hurlers through his career, but remembers a victory with an underdog UCD team as the Game of his Life.

★ **UCD:** J Conroy; P Dolan, M Cullen, T Finnegan; A Dunne, T Cronin, D O'Neill (0-4); **J Pilkington (0-1)**, B Carroll (0-1); T Maher (0-1), J Walsh, C O'Driscoll (0-3); E Scallan (0-3), S Hughes (0-1), J Byrne (2-7). Subs: D O'Mahoney for Cronin.

★ **UCC:** T Looney; D McInerney, A Murphy, F Lohan; K Murphy, P Kennealy, C Dillon; J Brennor (0-3), D Quigley; D O'Sullivan (0-1), A Brown (2-0), V O'Neill (0-1); D O'Mahony (0-1), T Doolan, G Maguire (1-8). Subs: P Hartnett for O'Sullivan, T O'Connell (1-0) for Dillon, O'Sullivan for K Murphy, K Murphy for Quigley.

THE ACTION

THE UNDERDOGS HAD their day in Waterford as the Fitzgibbon cup final rolled into town, and the tussle between UCD and UCC went down as one of the all-time classics. In the end it took extra-time to separate these two college strongholds, with the lesser known lights of UCD getting the job done in the end.

The win bridged a 14-year gap for the Dublin college. They started the game quite lamely, but came back into it before having to claw back a five-point deficit to force extra-time.

Wexford star Eamon Scallan chipped in with three points, while captain Jim Byrne shot the lights out with 2-7. But it was the all-action, free-willed Johnny Pilkington who ran the show in the middle of the field. The Offaly man dominated the game for the majority of the 90 minutes, chipped in with a point and led by example as the Dublin college showed immense grit and determination to get the better of their more accomplished opponents.

UCC played against the breeze in the opening half but they still had the craft and class to open up a 0-5 to 0-1 lead early on. UCD captain Jim Byrne pulled a goal back to make sure that the game didn't get away from them.

Turning to play with the wind in the second-half, the Cork men led by 1-8 to 0-9 and it looked like they were well set to kick for home. They extended their lead with goals from Gerry Maguire and Tom O'Connell, but UCD were still in with a fighters chance and driven on by Pilkington, they edged back closer and closer, until Scallan fired over to force extra-time.

Pilkington set up Jim Byrne for his second goal in the first period of extra-time to put UCD in the driving seat, and although Alan Browne got a goal back for UCC in the second period, UCD held firm and landed the title against the odds.

★★★★★

"

THERE ARE A number of games which stand out for me. Obviously, the 1995 Leinster final when I captained Offaly was a marvellous game... absolutely brilliant.

The 1998 club All-Ireland against Sarsfields was another game. I totally enjoyed that one, and got major benefit out of it, but the game that always comes back to me is the Fitzgibbon Cup final in 1993.

That's the one that makes me most proud.

I think it was my best game ever. The difference between that game and the other two games is that in the others, we had an awful lot of big players in it and, in this Fitzgibbon final, we didn't have too many big named players.

I think we had average kinds of club hurlers but just something special happened on that one given day, on that one given hour and, to me, it was a case that it doesn't make a difference who you are playing... that there is always that *chance*.

That's why I'm going with this game.

Now, on top of that as well, I had a very lacklustre grá at the time for Fitzgibbon hurling. College hurling didn't do an awful lot for me.

I went to UCG and played two years in Fitzgibbon down there. I enjoyed the company of the hurlers in it and we had great craic – the Fitzgibbon at that time was on a Friday, Saturday and Sunday. It was a weekend job.

When I went into college, actually it was the first time I came across circuit training; it was the first time I came across serious training to be fit for this three-day onslaught.

But I just couldn't take to college, and it didn't do anything for me.

I would have rather been at home with the boys in Birr, and maybe that was the problem. That time, it coincided with Birr having a bit of success as well and I just didn't gel there, but I went through the two years in UCG, and went onto UCD then.

In 1992, I played in the Fitzgibbon Cup and in '93 then, there wasn't anything spectacular about it. Again, lacklustre in terms of no real grá. I tried to get out of it... even thought of situations like, *I'll tell you what I'll do here, I can break my finger and that will get me out of the Fitzgibbon weekend.*

If I just break my small finger, that will do it.

I'd kind of go to training, and kind of not go to training... so the point of it all is that the colour of the jersey and the pride of the college just didn't do anything for me. It just wasn't there for me.

In 1992, we actually got to the Fitzgibbon final. We played UCC up in Belfast. Conal Bonnar and two or three other good lads were on the team.

We were beaten. It was the whole weekend, and there was banter and there was drinking, as you do... the whole lot. Bonnar and a few of the lads were devastated after ... they were after losing a Fitzgibbon Cup final, it was *just* a Fitzgibbon ... and I remember having a few pints and saying, 'Boys will ye stop, don't be worried about it!'

At this stage, now, Offaly were after losing to Antrim... and we had lost to Down. Birr had lost to Lusmagh in a county semi-final. I remember saying, 'Boys, to lose to Cork is a privilege'. The boys didn't see it that way.

It just didn't do anything for me.

So, 1993 anyway, I was still in UCD doing Agriculture and coming and going to training... missing training more than actually going to training. And again, as it turned out, my girlfriend at the time, she had a wedding on one weekend... and I said, 'Yeah, I'll be going to that wedding, there will be no problem!'

But then, as it turned out, the wedding clashed with the Fitzgibbon Cup weekend.

I suppose I could have turned around to them and said, 'Listen boys, I'm going to a wedding... I'm not around on the Saturday, but if ye make it through I'll be down!' At the same time, there was obviously some sort of allegiance, with me thinking, *How can I do this?*

So, my thinking was that I'd drive down, and I'd play the match. And if we lost, we are out of it, and I'm back up. That was the plan.

We'll go and see how the match goes.

If we lose, no big deal and I'll be back up for the evening part of the wedding.

As it turned out anyway, I went down... I drove down. We played, I think it was NIHE Limerick at the time and it was the worst game of hurling I ever played in. I have never seen two teams to want to lose a game as much as the two of us.

It was terrible. You could have taken off the six backs on both sides of the field and we would not have scored... and they wouldn't have scored! I think it ended up at about 11-10. It was atrocious.

I have to say my own attitude was probably worse than anyone's.

Anyway, we won by a point, and I thought, *F**k this anyway, what am I going to do now?* I decided to go back up and go back down the next morning. I rang my girlfriend and said, 'Listen, I'll be up, we're after winning... so I'll have to come back down in the morning'. The weekend was in Waterford.

It's only a two-hour journey.

So, I came up to the wedding and, look, it wasn't a mad night or anything like that. It was an *enjoyable* night. I wouldn't say I went in and horsed alcohol or anything like that. I got up the next morning, and my mother and father turned around and said, 'Here, listen, we'll go down with you to the match'.

We went down, and got into Waterford.

Now, at the time, UCD were staying in a hotel and I presumed they had their team meeting and their meal, and analysis and everything done. Myself and the parents went down and went into whatever hotel it was at the waterfront in Waterford. We had a bite to eat, and didn't I meet Jim O'Sullivan, who used to write with the *Examiner*... a Cork man.

At this stage I was after hurling three or four years with Offaly. UCC were after playing well against whoever they were playing in the semi-final and had won it well. They were fairly hot favourites to win the Fitzgibbon that year.

They had Pat Hartnett, who was playing centre-back. He had gone back to UCC to do dentistry. Hartnett had played in the 1986 All-Ireland final... and they had Cathal Casey, and two or three others.

We had your average Offaly lad and your Laois lad, and a couple of Kilkenny lads that were probably promising, but nothing major. We had a couple of Wexford lads too and a couple of Galway lads, but there wasn't anything outstanding about us.

O'Sullivan said to me, 'Well Johnny, ye are going to get a beating today'... or something along those lines. And I said, 'Jesus, I don't know about that, we'll have to wait and see!' But what he said stuck in my mind.

I went up and I met the lads.

I can't remember anything spectacular in the dressing-room or anything like that. The only thing about the game that stays with me as such, was that in the first 10 minutes, I did *nothing*.

The ball was kind of by-passing me. But from about 10 minutes on in the game, right to about five minutes left in the second-half of extra-time, I felt that I really controlled the game in the middle of the field. Looking back at it now, maybe I have rose tinted glasses or whatever, but it was a game that I completely dominated from the middle of the field.

I remember, we were four or five points down with maybe 10 minutes to play.

We had played well. Jim Byrne was our captain. He was in full-forward, and we were hitting balls in there... he played fierce well. I think he ended up scoring 2-7. But with five or 10 minutes to go, I can't remember exactly what was left, but we were a few points down still. Jimmy was in at kind of corner-forward/full-forward role. We got a free about 40 or 45 yards out and Jim was going to come out and take it. I turned around and said, 'Go back in there!'

And I shouted, 'Scallan, over here and take this free!' It was just kind of... take that free, put it over, get on with it... and get the next score. And that's what happened.

The college didn't matter to me, and the game itself didn't matter to me! But we were in a situation where we were four or five points down... and a game was there to be won.

We ended up drawing it and then, obviously, it went to extra-time, and we got on top and pulled away in the second-half. I think we were five or six points up in the last five minutes. I kind of died out then. I got a bit of a belt and just died out of the game.

Another thing that stands out is that I contributed to one of the greatest goals ever scored in Fitzgibbon. I had a ball and I kind of went to pull on it, and I remember some lad coming in with a challenge or something... and I half-hit it up in the air, about maybe 30 yards out from our own goal. And this Kerry lad, Browne I think was his name... he got it and he pulled on it first time... straight into the top corner of the net.

What an assist!!

UCD hadn't won it for a number of years. Afterwards, we had a few pints as well and I remember getting up on the bus and stopping off in Kilkenny.

We were playing in Waterford, and it was mid-term break in UCD. The previous year, we had come back from Belfast, and we had right craic on the day after around UCD.

But, because we were on mid-term, everybody just went off on their own after we'd won. It was *dead* after it, but the game itself stands out for me all on its own.

I think my own performance helped the whole team, because I was dominating in the middle of the field. Other lads played extremely well too. There was a Paul Maher from Tipperary, and Jim Byrne. There was Dan O'Neill from Kilkenny at wing back and he had a very good weekend. There was Padraig Dolan, and there were a couple of lads there from Killimor.

To be honest, and I am going to insult the lads here, but these weren't top senior club hurlers. These weren't anywhere really near inter-county. There were a couple of lads from Wexford… Eamonn Scallan played in the 1996 All Ireland final. There was an O'Keeffe, and a Liam Dunne, who would have been an older statesman at that time. I think he could have been 24 or 25 and had played with Laois and had played inter-county. There was also an O'Driscoll chap from Dublin.

It was just a funny bunch of lads, but it's a game I pick out.

If I go to the 1995 Leinster final with Kilkenny, John Troy is there and, in loads of ways, it's easier to play beside John Troy and Johnny Dooley because they see things. And if I go to the 1998 club All-Ireland… our club was strong at that time and Sarsfields, at the same time, were on their way down.

Whereas, in UCD, it was just a bunch of lads that really struck it lucky on the day and individually we all played well.

I told the UCD lads I was training with Offaly… and I told Eamon Cregan that I was training with UCD. The thing about it is that I was always naturally fit, so that was never going to be an issue of, 'Oh Jaysus, he's after putting on a pound or two'.

We are struggling here in Offaly and one of the reasons is… have we anyone on the Offaly panel making a mark in the Fitzgibbon Cup? There'd be a couple of them on the panel, as there always was, but at the end of it all there are very few hurlers from Offaly with a Fitzgibbon Cup medal.

Pat Fleury has one with UCG, and then there are two or three in Birr that have a medal, but not on the field of play. So it's a bit unique, that medal.

And then, I've another story about the actual medal presentation itself. They were giving out the medals anyway, and I happened to crash the car the day before. I made s**t of the car, so I didn't bother going up to get the medal.

About 10 years later, probably longer, a friend of mine who I was in college with, Padraic Dolan, arrived up to the house one day.

He had asked me, 'Are you around?'

'I am, yeah,' I told him.

And he arrived and said, 'I have something for you'. He handed me my Fitzgibbon medal.

'I was cleaning out my house!' he told me. 'I was moving, and I found your medal.' He had picked it up and brought it home about 15 or 20 years previous to that.

I have the medal in my home, and we'll have to put something special with it.

DAITHÍ REGAN
(JOHN TROY)

OFFALY 2-16 KILKENNY 2-5
Leinster SHC Final
Croke Park
JULY 16, 1995

Daithí Regan beats Ollie Baker in the 1995 All-Ireland final, the same season in which Offaly tore Kilkenny apart in the Leinster final.

★ **OFFALY:** D Hughes; S McGukian, K Kinahan, M Hanamy; B Whelahan (0-1), H Rigney, K Martin; J Pilkington (0-1), **D Regan (1-0)**; Johnny Dooley (0-3), **J Troy (0-2)**, Joe Dooley; B Dooley (0-4), P O'Connor (1-1), M Duignan (0-4). Subs: B Kelly for Joe Dooley, D Pilkington for Pilkington.

★ **KILKENNY:** M Walsh; E O'Connor, P Dwyer, L Simpson; M Keoghan, P O'Neill (0-1), W O'Connor; M Phelan, B Hennessy; PJ Delaney (0-1), J Power, A Ronan (0-3); E Morrissey, DJ Carey (2-0), D Byrne. Subs: D Gaffney for Phelan, C Brennan for Byrne, C Carter for Ronan.

THE ACTION

OFFALY CUT LOOSE on Kilkenny and won back-to-back Leinster titles as the wind and rain hurled around Croke Park. Atrocious weather conditions delayed the start of the match and, despite it being the middle of summer, supporters were forced to take refuge in the upper rows of the stands.

Once the game got going, a fired-up Offaly took matters into their own hands and avenged their National League semi-final defeat at the hands of the Cats. The reigning Leinster and All-Ireland champions hit top gear and, while they only led by two points at half-time, they really turned the screw in the second period.

The opening half was a low scoring affair, largely due to the weather conditions but it was Offaly who opened affairs from the versatile Michael Duignan. DJ Carey and Adrian Ronan were keeping Kilkenny motoring, but Offaly had the edge and a fine Johnny Pilkington point two minutes before half-time sent them in leading, 0-5 to 0-3.

The game-defining score came off the stick of trojan Offaly midfielder Daithí Regan. He took aim for a point from all of 50 yards after selling a lovely dummy, only for Kilkenny keeper Michael Walsh to drop it into the net to leave Offaly 1-6 to 0-3 in front.

Offaly drove home their advantage with points from John Troy, Billy Dooley and Brian Whelahan before the last nail was put in the Kilkenny coffin with just under 10 minutes to go.

Johnny Dooley sent in a long ball and, after sizing up the sliother from a good distance out, Pat O'Connor let fly, first time in mid-air, to shake the rain off the back of the net and complete the rout. Carey fired home a late consolation penalty but closing scores from John and Duignan gave Offaly an 11-point victory.

★★★★★

"

FOR ME, IT'S the 1995 Leinster final.

There was a big prelude to it. We had lost heavily to Kilkenny in the National League semi-final. There was a lot of talk about DJ Carey scoring his three goals against us in that game... a lot of talk about Kevin Kinahan being taken to task by DJ.

What people didn't realise was that there was a bit of a family accident in the week leading up to that game, and Kevin's mind wasn't on the game.

The criticism that Kevin got hurt us as a group and that league semi-final, looking back on it, it seemed to galvanise a belief within the media, and the hurling fraternity, that 1994 was a once-off for Offaly... that it was nice for us to win one.

Preceding that Leinster final then, the stakes were high.

It was all but an All-Ireland semi-final, with the greatest of respect to Down who were awaiting the winner.

Leading into the Leinster final, Éamonn Cregan really tapped into the national feeling that Kilkenny would not only beat us, but that they could really go to town on us.

It really dominated the preparation for us. The training for that game was ferocious. There was a real feeling in the group that we had been written-off and our achievement from 1994 had been pretty much rendered as a once-off.

I remember doing an interview with Liam Horan of the Independent before the final and while we were always told not to say a whole lot, I laced into him and said we were annoyed with how we were being treated. I was pretty bullish in that interview.

We were sick and tired of the agenda against us.

You could look back and say we over-hyped it, but it worked and we bought into it. Before that game, we had as much anger as I have ever seen from an Offaly team.

I carried a hamstring injury into the game, as well. I was getting treatment from Frances Daly up in Kildare. Frances would have been with us in Birr and was recognised as someone who would get you right for a game. Myself and John Troy were up with her and we missed the week's training leading into the game.

I had to do a fitness test up in Killeigh the day before the game. Andy Gallagher pulled into the car park to see how I was going. I was doing a couple of laps, and a bit of sprinting. When I started to pick up the pace a bit, I could start to feel the hamstring, so the doctor just said to me, 'Tell him that you're fine!'

The night before the game then, I was in the worst form because I was terrified that the hamstring was going to go. I stayed with my brother that night in Dublin.

We went down to Lonergan's, which was an off-shoot of the Montrose Hotel. My two brothers were living in Dublin... so we were all there. The boys were having a few pints and I was having a mineral. No one knew who we were, but I just wanted to get out of there... I was in the foulest of form.

The following morning, we met in The Ashling Hotel. The bus pulled in and I will never forget the atmosphere. There was something different about it, no chat or craic... and then we had a team meeting.

It was the greatest team meeting that I was ever at in my life. Éamonn captured the whole mood perfectly. Éamonn and a few more would normally say a few words, but he actually threw the meeting open to everybody.

He spoke about Kilkenny trying to isolate Kevin Kinahan and DJ Carey, but he didn't come up with the solution; he challenged the group and asked for our views.

Everyone just got vested into the whole thing and everyone fed off one another. When we left the hotel to go to Croke Park, it was the quietest bus. Normally there would be a bit of craic... but there wasn't a sound. We started to realise that Kilkenny had no idea what was going to hit them that day.

We really hated Kilkenny back then, even though we had so much respect for them and their hurling. We were going to take our anger out on them.

An extraordinary thing happened the previous week before the team was announced at training on the Tuesday night. And I don't know if it ever got out. I don't know if Kevin Kinahan ever found out... but his two corner-backs and his goalkeeper know this story.

The management were very concerned about Kevin's pace against DJ, and the whole league semi-final episode.

Joe Errity was training very well at full-back on the 'possibles' team in our training games and the night that the team was announced, Derry O'Donovan, our coach, went to Errity and told him that he was going to be starting.

The management called David Hughes, Shane McGukian and Martin Hanamy together, and had a bit of chat with them and told them they were worried about Kevin and a lack of pace... and that they were going to go with Joe at full-back.

The boys told the management that while they knew Joe was going well and that he was a fantastic hurler, there was no way they were taking Kevin out of there.

So, that changed the plans, and as they came back into the dressing-room to announce the team nobody had got to Joe to tell him about the change of plan. He was sitting there waiting for his name to be announced.

Joe, being the model professional, didn't kick up a song and dance about it, which was another sign of the great player that he was.

Myself and Brendan Kelly were in the dressing-room before the game. The rest of the lads were out watching the minor match.

I had five hurls beside me ready to go and ready to be used, and in walks Mícheál Ó Muircheartaigh. A really lovely man... we had a bit of a chat. He saw the five hurls and we had a bit of a laugh about whether I was going to use the five of them, because back in those times you broke a lot more hurls.

He wandered over to Brendan Kelly then and there was a bit of small-talk about the game and Brendan turned around to him and asked Mícheál who he thought would win the game? Mícheál said that he would probably have to give an edge to Kilkenny after the league semi-final.

He barely had the words out of his mouth and Kelly was telling him to get out of the dressing-room. I remember thinking that was a harsh thing to say to a man like that, but doesn't that go to show you where Brendan Kelly's head was at! There was no way he was going to accept from anyone that we were going to be beaten.

It spoke volumes about where we were and, looking back on it, I'd have admiration for Brendan, as you look for small little things from a mentality point of view.

Then there was the whole issue of the deluge of rain that had taken place before the game. We were absolutely wired going out on the pitch.

Johnny Pilkington was first out, Martin Hanamy was second and, I remember,

I was third. I remember Hanamy roaring at Johnny to turn around and we all huddled in.

'They wouldn't send Kilkenny out in that weather!' Martin roared... 'Get back into the dressing-room!'

The stewards were trying to get us to go out.

Cregan fed into it straight away. The message was that not only had we been disrespected since the All-Ireland the previous year, not only had we been disrespected since the league semi-final... but now they want to put us out first when we should be second because of being All-Ireland champions.

Next thing, the door was being knocked on. They were telling us that we had thrown RTE and their timings out of sync.

Cregan just got a hurl and slammed it off a table.

'We will go when we are ready!

'And no one is going to tell us what to do today.'

I remember going out onto the pitch then, and no one was going to reason with us. We were gone past rational thinking. Even though we gave them a hiding, we were only two points up at half-time. But coming in at half-time, we knew we were going to win.

It didn't matter what they brought.

The fire was burning so hard inside of us, but the message at half-time was so calm. It was all about what we were doing and the battles we were winning. Everyone was so focused.

I can safely say that no one played bad that day. I can remember Michael Duignan, Johnny Pilkington and Pat O'Connor slagging the likes of Eddie and Willie O'Connor. Stuff that wasn't done before. Our lads had no fear. We weren't a confrontational group but, that day, we had no problem letting them know we were not afraid. I remember Titch Phelan in the second-half looking at me in a funny way... just a look of, Jesus, we weren't expecting this!

Even when we were giving them lessons in the 80's and early 90's, it never dulled their belief that they were better than us, and that's what makes them such a successful county.

Eddie O'Connor came out with a ball in the second-half and he over-carried it. Dickie Murphy blew him for it, and Eddie did a bit of a jig on the field in frustration and belted the ball into the Cusack Stand. John Troy started patting him on the back and winking at him… driving him mental.

We had given them beatings before, but this one was being administered with harshness to it.

Pat O'Neill was roaring up to his forwards at one stage, trying to get them going and John Troy just turned to him and told him he would have to go up himself as they were at nothing up there.

There was no easing up either, because we had so much fire there that day. We conceded two goals at the end but it was an extraordinary game.

There wasn't a bother with the hamstring either. But I genuinely thought the night before the game that I wouldn't make it.

The Offaly supporters that day as well were unreal. They all congregated in the middle of the Hogan Stand, as the Cusack wasn't covered in at the time and they moved over to avoid getting wet. The noise they made that day was unbelievable.

It was probably the only time ever after a game that I didn't go out after it. Everyone celebrates differently but, for me, I wanted to stay at home… I didn't want to ruin the memory or the feeling of it. That brought us even closer together.

Éamonn Cregan was incredible. He knew how to tap into everything. He took no bullshit from anyone and we hung on his words. He also believed in our style of hurling.

Back then, we all loved our ground hurling drills. When we were on song at training, that ball would hum… and we were moving that ball up and down the field at huge speed.

Everything that was in us as hurlers came out that day. Practically every one of us had the game of our lives that day. I'd say anyone that was involved would have the 1995 Leinster final in their top three.

To know in a dressing-room, and for all your colleagues to know, that you were going to win a game before you even go out onto the field… that was an extraordinary thing to have to our advantage before a Leinster final.

They hadn't a hope of beating us that day, and I wouldn't have felt like that before any other game with Kilkenny.

❞

JOHN TROY

John Troy celebrates hitting the back of the net against Kilkenny in the 1998 Leinster final.

❝

WE WERE ALL-IRELAND champions coming into the game, but Kilkenny were favourites to win. The reason for that was they beat us in the league semi-final in Thurles by six points. I often look at games and try to balance out the scores.

We conceded four goals that day, something we normally didn't do. It was 4-8 to 0-14, so we scored twice more in the game than they did. Back then, we didn't really concede goals – later on in the 90s we did concede goals against Kilkenny, but that wasn't the backs fault, it was Kilkenny at the time... and anything inside 40 yards, they were going at it hard for goals and maybe as a forward division we weren't working hard enough out the field.

Being underdogs was the first significant thing about the win that day. The second thing was, I got injured against Wexford in the semi-final. Now that was a strange game… it was played at 6pm on a Sunday evening.

I don't know why it was at that time, but there was a great crowd at it on a real warm evening.

The previous year we had hurled Wexford in the Leinster final and I was playing centre-forward on Liam Dunne. However, Wexford had changed up their team in 1995 and I was marking George O'Connor.

George hadn't hurled the year before and looking at George through the 80s, he was an idol… if you want to call him that.

We were hurling into Hill 16 in the first-half that evening. We were standing for the National Anthem. I looked over at George and here was this perfect specimen of a man. He was obviously after getting a good rub from the physio before the game, and he was all brown and shining and about a foot taller than me.

I said to myself, *Holy Jaysus!!*

I remember, just before half-time I pulled my calf muscle. I don't know what the doctor did to it at half-time but I played on anyway and finished up inside, in corner-forward.

I didn't actually do any hurling training from the Leinster semi-final to the final. The only training I did was with Joachim Kelly. Joachim was a selector and he used to bring me down to Templemore once during the week, and again on a Saturday, to go swimming in the garda place.

He had another lad there and he used to put me through circuit training. I wouldn't have been used to that, all that upper body stuff and I said to myself, *The sooner I'm back running, the better!*

I did a small fitness test then with Daithí Regan, who was also injured, but we were picked to play anyway.

I remember watching the minor game.

It was a beautiful day. Kilkenny beat our minors, and we went in and togged out.

We did our speeches and whatever and, as we ran out onto the field, it started bucketing rain. We ran across and got the photograph taken, but Martin Hanamy said, 'Come on lads, we are going in out of this!'

Our jerseys were hanging with the wet.

By the time we did get out and got going, we were fired up. Myself and Pat

O'Neill had a bit of a run in about two minutes into the game. It was my own fault... Dickie Murphy warned me.

I would have hurled on Pat during underage. I hurled on him in the semi-final in 1994 as well. Pat O'Neill was a tough hurler, but wasn't a dirty hurler. He could give it and he could take it.

It was a tough game. It wasn't an overly skilful game but there was no hiding place. Johnny Dooley got a bad belt into the face in the first-half. It was a deliberate blow.

That got us riled up even more.

Half-time came, and we went back in. Éamonn Cregan was a good man and a good man to motivate. If you weren't doing your job, he would tell you straight to your face too.

He said that we had a real chance of setting the books right with these lads. 'Everything is suiting them', he said. 'The conditions are suiting them because they are not as good as you... but we'll only let the conditions suit them if we allow it to suit them.'

For five or six minutes of the second-half, it was more of the same as the opening half, nothing overly dramatic.

Daithí Regan got a goal then, that went in off Michael Walsh and, for the next 25 minutes, it was as good a place as you could ever be as a hurler. Things opened up for us.

Billy Dooley was like he was in the 1994 All-Ireland. He got three points from play, I got two points, Brian Whelahan got a super score from wing back, Johnny Dooley got one from a free and from play... and Duignan got a point... and Pat O'Connor got 1-1. They were all good quality scores.

I wouldn't say we didn't often play as a team, but that day we really did *play* as a team. If a lad was in a bad position, he looked for somebody else.

At one stage in that game we were 13 or 14 points ahead.

Kilkenny came back late on and got a few goals but, when you look back on it, we beat Kilkenny in a Leinster final by 11 points.

If you look back through our history of winning nine Leinster senior hurling titles, we only beat Kilkenny in three of them. We beat them by a point in 1980, three points in '89... and now 11 points in 95'.

We wouldn't have thought we would beat them by 11 points... not even against the worst Kilkenny team would you expect to do that.

For those 25 minutes in the second-half, it was unbelievable. Croke Park can be the greatest place on earth when you're winning but the total opposite when you're not.

Eddie O'Connor was a big talking point that day too. Eddie came in for a lot of rough treatment that day, but he looked for it himself.

There was one situation when the ball broke in behind him. He was just about to rise the ball and Pat O'Connor came and met him with a shoulder... putting him out over the sideline.

Pat was still standing but when Eddie was still on the ground, he drew a boot on Pat. It just happened that Éamonn Cregan was standing there. Éamonn must have said something to the ref, and when Eddie O'Connor got up, he hit Éamonn Cregan a shoulder.

In fairness to Cregan, he just put his hands up and walked away.

But just as he was walking away, Andy Gallagher came running down the sideline and started giving out to O'Connor. Eddie grabbed the ball and threw it at the two boys and they just ducked in time. It was fierce funny looking back on it.

Then Eddie took off the helmet and threw it on the ground.

I finished up marking him inside at corner-forward. A ball came inside, he gathered it, went to go one way but turned back around and, just as he came back my way, I knew I wasn't going to get him but I snigged him on the elbow with the hurl.

Next thing the whistle went and I thought it was for a free out, but Dickie Murphy had pulled him up for over-carrying. I must have said something to him... he went to bury the ball at me and just missed. He was a brilliant hurler as well.

DJ Carey was there, and Denis Byrne was the new kid on the block. DJ got three goals in that league semi-final in Thurles and Kevin Kinahan was under huge pressure coming into that Leinster final marking him.

DJ did get a penalty, but the game was done at that stage. Kevin Kinahan was a big-game player and very solid playing in the hardest position on the field.

Johnny Pilkington had a great final too. He might not have always got Man of the Match but he was always in the top three. He was captain as well and had we won the All-Ireland that year, it would have been unique for him as he captained Birr to the club All-Ireland earlier in 1995.

I actually hadn't realised that until I watched his episode of *Laochra Gael* recently.

I was interviewed after the game by Marty Morrissey and he passed a comment about it being easy... but it was far from easy.

I was wondering what the papers were going to write after the game. The papers can motivate you. I remember another incident in 1998 when Michael Bond took over. Pete Finnerty wrote an article and said Offaly would be as well off ringing in sick today before we played Clare in the first of the three games.

That Leinster final was definitely the most satisfying victory of my senior career.

Kilkenny were not an old team. They won All-Irelands in 1992 and '93... and they were going for three in-a-row in '94.

We hurled Railway Cup in late 1993 or early '94 in Nowlan Park. Eddie O'Connor was captain and we were back in Langtons after it, having the dinner when Eddie stood up and thanked everyone. But then he said at the end, 'The dream is still on, the three in-a-row is still on!'

There were lads from Offaly, Wexford and Dublin in the room as well, so that was good motivation for us in 1995. That's the kind of character Eddie was, he always said what was on his mind.

The only sad thing was that we didn't go on and win an All-Ireland in 1995.

To be fair, I know we missed chances, but when you look back on Clare's All-Ireland in 1995, they missed their chances too. I think the best team won that one on the day.

1987 was special for me as well, when I won my first minor All-Ireland. I was only 16, playing in goals. Brian Whelahan, Johnny Dooley and Adrian Cahill, Lord have mercy on him, were 16 as well... the four of us played that day.

I was a sub in 1986 as well. Joe Errity was in goals but moved out centre-back in 1987. I got to play in 10 All-Ireland finals with Offaly, between minor, under-21 and senior. In 1989 I played in the minor final when we beat Clare, and a week later played in the under-21 final against Tipperary.

We utilised a lot of players from those minor teams and there weren't too many lads who didn't get a fair chance. There wasn't much experience back then. If you were beaten, you were gone; that didn't change until 1998. We look back at 1998 when we played eight championship games and thought it was mad… but it is the norm nearly at this stage.

I will tell you the truth. There were lots of heated training sessions. Lots of incidents down at training that lads would get six months for! But it was healthy in a way, and once it was over… it was over. I often look back and think of players that would have drifted away; the likes of Roy Mannion and Adrian Cahill come to mind.

Adrian Cahill was a natural. He got trials in England for soccer and was very close to getting a contract. The famous Joe Jordan was very impressed with him. I have a memory card of him and I look at it every now and again.

I came onto the senior team in 1990 and was a sub. I was a sub again in 1991. Lads would say to me… 'Ah, it was alright for you, you were one of the Troys'… but I spent two and a half years before I got a championship match.

I always liked to play in the central positions. Anywhere I could get involved fairly quick. That time, goalkeepers would always puck the ball up the middle… and I wanted to be in the thick of it.

I remember, we had a meeting before the Leinster semi-final in 1994 and Éamonn Cregan asked Jim Troy where he was going to puck the balls out too?

Jim said he was going to put the first one down the middle, the second one out to left and the third out to the right… and wherever the ball stayed the longest, and wasn't coming back up the field… that's where he would keep pucking it.

There was no arguing with that.

BRIAN WHELAHAN

BIRR 0-12 CLARECASTLE 0-11
(after extra time)
All-Ireland Club SHC Semi-Final Replay
Thurles
FEBRUARY 28, 1998

Brian Whelahan in action against Clare in the All-Ireland semi-final in 1998 and (inset) he celebrates victory in the All-Ireland Club Championship earlier in that emotional season for Birr.

★ **BIRR:** B Mullins; S Whelahan, J Errity, G Doorley; Barry Whelahan, **Brian Whelahan (0-1)**, N Claffey; J Pilkington (0-1), C Hanniffy; D Hanniffy (0-4), G Hanniffy, G Cahill (0-4); L Power, D Pilkington, O O'Neill. Subs: D Regan (0-2) for Power, P Carroll for O'Neill, C McGlone for G Hanniffy, K Spillane for Carroll.

★ **CLARECASTLE:** T Hegarty; G Canny, M Sheedy, B Scanlon; P Healy (0-1), S Sheedy, A Daly (0-1); V O'Loughlin, K Morrissey; R Fitzgerald, F Tuohy, D Scanlon (0-1); A Neville (0-1), K Ralph (0-5), G O'Loughlin (0-2). Subs: J Healy for Morrissey, O Plunkett for Fitzgerald, D Fitzgerald for G O'Loughlin, R Fitzgerald for Plunkett, G O'Loughlin for V O'Loughlin, K Morrissey for D Fitzgerald.

THE ACTION

IT TOOK EXTRA-TIME, after a replay, but Birr finally got the job done and disposed of Clarecastle to set up an All-Ireland club final with Sarsfields of Galway on St Patrick's Day.

Both the drawn game and the replay were real wars of attrition, with the Birr men just having enough in the end to get over the line. Brian Whelahan gave an exhibition at centre-back on a day when he came in for some heavy treatment. Clarecastle had three players booked for fouls on him.

It was a day of mixed emotions in Thurles. From the elation of winning a war against the Clare champions, to the news coming through that club stalwart Tommy Errity, father of captain Joe and sub goalkeeper Martin, had passed away prior to the match.

Playing against the strong wind in the opening half, Birr were wasteful and nine first-half wides contributed to them trailing 0-6 to 0-4 at the break. Crucially, Birr made a decent start to the second-half with Darren Hanniffy clipping over his and Birr's third point, while half-time substitution Daithí Regan drew a foul for Gary Cahill to point from a free.

It was all-Birr at this stage and they soon led 0-7 to 0-6 with points from Gary Cahill (two) and Regan. Wind assisted and with the momentum, all the signs pointed to them pulling away but they failed to score for the remainder of normal time. Ken Ralph landed the levelling score from a free and extra-time ensued.

Birr led 0-10 to 0-8 at half-time in extra-time with points from Brian Whelahan ('65') and Cahill, but it was tight and tense hurling. Ralph cut the gap to the minimum, but a trademark solo run point from Johnny Pilkington restored their two-point cushion.

Clarecastle had another kick in them and two points, the pick of those from Anthony Daly, levelled the drama-filled game. Then with two minutes to go, Regan fired over the winner to end an energy-sapping day.

★★★★★

"

I SUPPOSE, FROM our point of view, we had won a club All-Ireland in 1995 and then it was like as if the whole bottom fell out of our world. We were beaten later that year by Clareen by a point in the Offaly semi-final, and really went into a major decline then the following year in 1996 when St Rynagh's beat us in the semi-final.

There was an awful lot of seeds sown there. Later that year in 1996, we played a league semi-final against Kilcormac and we hadn't 15 to start… after winning a club All-Ireland 18 months prior! I will never forget that time.

My dad came in as trainer and the first thing he decided to do was, he started to bring in a whole lot of young players.

My brother Simon had been there under Padraig Coen. Barry had played in 1996 alright but the likes of Niall Claffey, the Hanniffys… all these guys started to get a major look-in and dad decided to transform the set-up and go with a young team.

We beat Clareen in the final in 1997. They were going for three in-a-row, so they were at their best and we ended up going through Leinster then. I won't say comfortably, but I never thought we were going to lose any of the games. We beat Castletown in the final… which turned out to be a huge rivalry in the making with Castletown.

Clarecastle came out of Munster then. Anthony Daly was on the team. They had three players and a couple of panellists… Daly, Sparrow O'Loughlin, Fergie Tuohy… they were all part of that Clare 1995 breakthrough team.

And we had our guys!

From the time both teams won their provincial finals, all I can say is from this side of the fence, the whole Clare thing started to build… and I mean *really* build. We trained very, very hard for them, I'll never forget it.

My dad had a way of playing two games at weekends, Saturday and Sunday. He was the first really to go looking at playing inter-county teams and he followed that on. He was part of our set-up in 1991 when we played Clare in a practice game, so he decided to go after teams that were back in training. We started back training on St Stephen's Day… he got us together for maybe 40 minutes and he said, 'Go and enjoy yourselves because this will be the end of it!'

We actually trained in the rugby field across from the hurling field, doing all of our physical training. We were ploughing through the field… you would think, *Did someone have a permanent hose on the field?* It was real muck and dirt.

The pressure going into that game! Like, I've always felt nerves before a game, and I've always enjoyed the nerves in the sense that I felt I had to be nervous. But, I felt *real* pressure in this game. I knew a lot of things would be defined by this game.

I'll never forget it… we had a meeting before it and a lot of players broke down. They had trained so hard and had invested so much time into that preparation. The team was named… lads were left off and it got very intense, but that sort of added to the whole occasion as well. Because these lads, if it meant that much to them and they weren't starting… then the lads that did start better seize their opportunity!

We always had a good Offaly following going through Leinster, and it was fantastic. People came from all over the county cheering us on, and it was more an Offaly thing than a Birr thing. As they might say themselves, it shortened the winter for them!

The support arrived in Thurles that day for us, with Offaly caps being worn! And I think the same could be said for Clare.

Whatever it was, there just seemed to be that hangover from 1995. And the feeling at the time was that a Clare team had an edge over an Offaly team at whatever level, and that we had probably shot our bolt.

I felt we were the better team for most of game. We just didn't convert our scores. I know Darren Hanniffy probably ran the legs off Anthony Daly that day, but it just didn't convert into scores for us and there was quite a breeze blowing. But in both halves, I think both teams played their best hurling against the wind.

We went in only a point or two up at half-time after hurling with the wind, after being dominant… and we were just thinking, *Oh my God!*

The second-half was a serious, *serious* battle.

Fergie Tuohy was playing wing forward on Niall Claffey, and Niall actually had an outstanding game… like he had all year. He was the man that was designated that year to pick up anyone that was on either of the wings. He picked up Johnny

Dooley in the county final that year, and to be given that task at such a young age was unbelievable, to be honest.

I felt we had weathered the storm and then, out of the blue, just near the end… a ball broke in. I don't know how it bloody happened, but it ended up in the net. The game changed and we were a point down.

It more or less looked like we were going to be knocked out of the championship… we were going to be *gone*.

Daithí Regan and Oisin O'Neill were brought on and they both got a score to draw the game. It went to a replay, and that even added bloody more tension. The feeling coming out after was that we had probably been the better team, but they were more economical and if they got a period of dominance that we enjoyed the first day, they would probably win comfortably enough.

Ken Ralph was on the frees for them; he was from Tipperary, and he missed nothing that year. As I said, Sparrow was there, and they had Victor O'Loughlin too, and I think he was a panellist in 1995… so these lads were all seasoned campaigners.

My dad made one or two changes the following day. He brought on Garech Doorley at corner-back, because Brian Hennessy was carrying a hamstring injury into the first game and he struggled.

Garech came in and he had the legs, so he snuffed out that issue… that corner-forward issue. We were actually even more dominant the second day and it was actually like déjà vu… we could not score, just *couldn't* score.

I'll never forget coming in at half-time and Anthony Daly rallying the troops.

'We have them… THEY'RE F***ED NOW!' he shouted.

'They're f***ed now lads, they're not able to beat us and we will take them in the second-half!'

It was nip and tuck the whole way. We actually played with the wind in the second-half and couldn't get ahead. It was such an eerie feeling; it was wide after wide. We were just waiting for Sparrow to come into it because he had been so quiet in the first game… and I thought, *If this lad does get going, we could be in trouble.*

Luckily enough, that didn't transpire. But they had enough lads around the field chipping away. It was the whole Clare thing at the time… they were fighting on their backs. The referee blew the final whistle.

It was a draw match, again... it was going for extra-time.

It was the only time I ever felt we possibly weren't going to win the game, because we had hurled with the wind in the second-half, but we actually got the point to draw the game. We came in and my father brought in Daithí... and I'll never forget it.

The first thing he did was he had a rattle at Anthony Daly, and it was important. It was very *important* that Daithí played that role for us.

There were a lot of lads out on their feet, but lads were going on adrenaline. I had my brother Barry playing wing back beside me, and I had Simon playing corner-back along with Niall Claffey. Then you had Garreth Doorley, and you had Joe Errity full-back.

You had huge energy all around, and you knew at that stage... these boys were 19, 20 and 21 years of age, they weren't going to be failing.

In fairness, with the three Hanniffys... you had Conor, Darren and Gary, all young men. It was the one thing I suppose over the whole course of that year, that the team was able to stay going, and *stay* going, and I just felt that if my dad had stayed with the tried and tested of the couple of years before, we would have run out of steam. And in that game we definitely would have been beaten.

These lads were absolutely hungry for success.

They weren't a team that had won underage; I think Simon said he only won one underage medal. They just couldn't wait to get up to senior and be given an opportunity to have a go and be successful, and that year, during those moments, I think they actually were the ones that brought us through.

It was hugely rewarding. When Daithí put the ball over the bar to win the game and the whistle was blown, there was such emotion. And then, within the space of a minute and a half, word came through... Joe Errity's dad had passed away in the stand and we didn't know what way to be.

I will never forget, we waited in the tunnel for Joe to come in. His brother Martin had gone to tell him; Martin was our sub goalie. The two of them came in and they were in bits, and we were just there with our heads down.

I'll never, ever forget it.

Their chairman came in and spoke for about 10 minutes. It put everything into real respective. Tommy never missed training and I'd say he was at more training sessions than most of the players... he was there every night.

He was a Coolderry man, who had won numerous county finals with Coolderry and when you went down training... Tommy was there!

He was there every night, hurling was a major part of his life. The Clarecastle players and club paid great gestures and respect, and they came up for the funeral. They came in and had a few drinks in my pub after and it just shows what GAA is really about at the end of the day.

Joe missed the first week of training obviously after it.

Then, we were training one night over in the field. We had trained hard and we went in to get a shower. My father said to everyone, 'Don't go for a minute, I want to see ye'.

He went and he opened the door, and he said, 'Now lads, I've someone very important here to speak to ye!'

And Joe's mam came in. She thanked everyone for the support the family received over the previous few days... but she continued the tradition of not missing a training session until the year was over.

'He might not be here physically,' she said. 'But I can tell ye, he'll be here and we'll be there!' And they never missed a training session.

I think everyone came out of that training session and we all knew what we had to do, but there wasn't even a word spoken. That was it.

We went into that final. We were playing Joe Cooney's team, Sarsfields who had won back-to-back All-Ireland titles. I think they were the first team to do it... and household names all over the place. I can honestly say I was in no fear of losing that game even though we were playing them.

We were on a mission, we knew what had to be done with everything that had happened... the year that had happened, and we went out that day and we won by seven or eight points. Joe Errity gave one of the most amazing speeches after the game, full of emotion as well. It was just an unbelievable few weeks.

Daithí Regan's first game to start that year for Birr was the All-Ireland final, after getting the winning point in the semi-final. There are unbelievable memories in that little pocket of a few weeks for a lot of lads from different points of view. I can honestly say that I never felt the pressure of a game as much in my life, as

I felt in that game... until Thurles later that year. It happened to be Clare again.

You could sense the intensity; we could even get it when we went into Hayes' Hotel before the match... and the crowd outside it. We really didn't experience that before because normally we were kept away.

If we were playing in Croke Park, we'd go to the Lucan Spa and there would only be a few people there. Or we'd go to The Ashling Hotel, but now we were in the middle of Thurles in Hayes' Hotel where everyone goes... and the crowd was just unbelievable.

It was a fine day. Pat O'Connor told me he was walking over the bridge, and he said there wasn't a word spoken.

Everyone was there. It was like as if they were all going to hurl, and he said once you arrived at the ground, you could sense that. It was the first time I'd ever experienced Thurles packed.

I would have hurled in a league quarter-final or a league semi-final with maybe 20,000 people in it, but never with 50,000 and such a background to a game... with people baying for victory on both sides. That made the occasion that bit more special as well.

JOHNNY DOOLEY

OFFALY 1-15 WEXFORD 0-17
Leinster SHC Semi-Final
Croke Park
JUNE 14, 1998

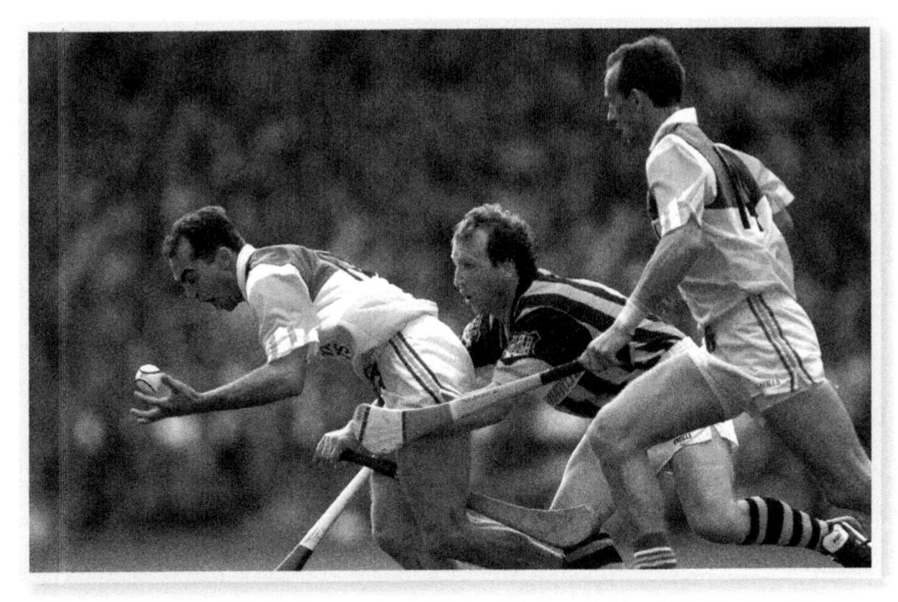

Johnny Dooley breaks away from Willie O'Connor of Kilkenny in the 1998 All-Ireland final.

★ **OFFALY:** S Byrne; Barry Whelahan, H Rigney, M Hanamy; C Cassidy, Brian Whelahan (0-3), K Martin; J Pilkington (0-1), G Hanniffy; **Johnny Dooley (1-3)**, M Hand, M Duignan; J Troy (0-5), B Dooley (0-1), Joe Dooley (0-1). Subs: C Farrell for Hand, J Ryan for G Hanniffy, P Mulhare (0-1) for Joe Dooley.

★ **WEXFORD:** D Fitzhenry; C Kehoe, G Cushe, E Furlong; D Ruth, L O'Gorman, S Flood; A Fenlon (0-1), R Hassey; R McCarthy (0-1), M Storey (0-4), M Jordan (0-1); T Dempsey, L Murphy (0-1), P Codd (0-9). Subs: B Byrne for Dempsey, J Purcell for Jordan.

THE ACTION

OFFALY HAD TO draw on all their experience before striking at the death to get one over on Wexford and advance to the Leinster final. Babs Keating's charges looked like they would be heading for an early exit from the championship until a late goal from Johnny Dooley snatched victory from the jaws of defeat, to earn a below-par Offaly a shot at Kilkenny in the final.

Johnny Dooley was making his first appearance of the championship having missed the opening round win over Meath with a broken thumb, but showed no signs of it, notching 1-3 and turning provider on numerous other occasions.

The teams were deadlocked at 0-3 each on 12 minutes, before Wexford began to gain the upper-hand and went into a two point lead despite their wide-count starting to rack up. Johnny Dooley looked to be sending Offaly in ahead at half-time only for Martin Storey to equalise as the teams retired level at 0-9 apiece.

The second-half began with an early exchange of scores, before Wexford hit a purple patch and went four points clear. Martin Storey clipped over a score before three points from Paul Codd (two frees) had the Wexford men with the finish-line in sight.

However, Offaly stood defiant, and Wexford began to wilt. Whelahan, John Troy and Paudie Mulhare all landed points to cut the lead to the minimum. Paul Codd's ninth point of the day pushed Wexford back two in front and to what seemed a Leinster final, but Offaly came knocking again.

A Brian Whelahan 'hit and hope' free was deflected out for a '65' and with the same ploy, Whelahan lobbed it in again. This time, as the ball broke, waiting was Johnny Dooley, who let fly with a first-time shot on the ground that evaded the packed goalmouth and hit the net.

★★★★★

"

I GOT INJURED in the lead-up to the game. I was playing with my club in a league game against Kilcormac/Killoughey and I fractured my thumb in two places and that left me in a cast for six-to-eight weeks.

I had no game-time. I was off work, so I went running three times a week. Back then, you wouldn't be given a set programme by the physio or anything like that. There is a little pitch across the road from where I live, and I used to do two- or three-kilometre runs along with sprints, and all that.

The one thing I didn't want coming up to the match was not being fit; it was bad enough not having game-time under my belt; I didn't want to be behind fitness-wise as well.

I was always gearing myself back for that Wexford game.

I got back training with the panel the week before the game. The management team were happy at where my fitness was at; I was well up with the group when it came to the sprinting at training.

I had no hurling done in the six weeks leading up to the game though - I only started back on the Tuesday night before the semi-final.

I wanted to make an impression that night and I think I did, as I was selected to play. I remember thinking to myself that I was going to have to really make my mark that night because I was in danger of not making the starting team. Paudie Mulhare was looking like he might get in ahead of me.

Heading into the game, of course I was a bit nervous having not had any competitive hurling in me. Also, it was the first time in seven years where I was facing into a game where I wasn't on the frees. John Troy had hit them against Meath in the opening round win and did well, so it was an unusual position to be in.

Wexford were going for three in-a-row of Leinster titles and there was this 200-year anniversary of the invasion of the South – a massive event for Wexford. They were building it up to be their year!

It was a Leinster semi-final, but there were 46,000 people in Croke Park that day. We had Babs Keating over us and there was a bit of hype about that as well.

From our side, training was going particularly well but we weren't playing well. We were flying it fitness-wise, but our hurling wasn't good.

On that particular day, we didn't play as well as we would have liked; we were stuttering our way through the game. Wexford ran up a good number of wides in both the first- and second-half and, realistically, they could have put us away. But we just kept hanging in.

I remember, I got a couple of points in the first-half, but it was a real battle... a struggle. We had three or four new guys on the team as well. Colm Cassidy, Mark Hand and Barry Whelahan were all new. Our team was changing up at this stage.

In the second-half, Wexford looked like they were going to pull away. They got four points ahead on a few occasions, but we always kept it to that four points.

I got a point with about 15 minutes to go... and I threw out two balls, one to John Troy and one to Paudie Mulhare. We were still hanging in.

Time was up and we were still two points down. Brian Whelahan stood over a free and I remember saying to myself that I was going to get in around the square for it. We knew it was the last play of the game. Sid (Brian Whelahan) floated it in around the edge of the square... and the ball hopped.

To this day, I can still remember clearly the ball hopping down in front of me. There was a cluster of legs around the place and I just said I was going to get some sort of contact on this.

The ball just produced itself in the right spot. My shot could have hit a leg or a hurl, but it flew into the corner of the net. It was an unbelievable feeling and I don't mind saying this... but it was ahead of the 1994 All-Ireland final for me.

I played a better game in 1998 and, in its own right, it was equally as important. From the point of view... a defeat and our season was over.

A lot of the Offaly players would put their hands up and admit that it wasn't their best game and that happens, but I was happy with my performance and contributed about 1-7 between winning frees and setting up scores and all that.

I got a lot of personal satisfaction from that game. John Troy was still on the frees and he continued hitting them for the rest of the year. I was trying to get back on the frees but, in fairness to John, he wasn't doing anything wrong and the management were going on form.

We had a good night after too. We pulled up in Leixlip and we went in and had a few pints, before we went back to Tullamore.

Offaly supporters didn't travel in massive numbers that day. At the time, it was the biggest attendance ever at a Leinster semi-final. I'd say 35,000 of the 46,000 there were from Wexford. Wexford is a huge hurling county.

There was an added incentive that time because there was no back door or second chance. Fair enough, if you got to a Leinster final you got a second chance but, if we lost that semi-final, we were *gone.*

Wexford were in the top two or three teams in the country at the time and we had the feeling going home that evening that we had taken out a *big* team without playing our best. We just did enough to get over the line.

There was a cockiness about Wexford as well.

We had beaten them in 1994 and '95, but lost to them in '96 and '97... and this would have been three in-a-row for them. They were getting the upper-hand on us.

That win catapulted us forward and we beat them the next four years after that. It was a pivotal moment and I think that game took a lot from the Wexford lads. They were an ageing team and were making one big push.

The season that unfolded after that? Well, no one could have predicted what was going to happen. Babs would eventually leave before the three Clare games and all that. My injury woes would continue though. We played Kilkenny in a challenge match after the Leinster final and I broke my cheek-bone. I had to get 16 stitches on the left side of my face.

I was having a stop-start year with the injuries, but I got back in time for the Clare games.

We ended up winning the All-Ireland, but we also won the county title with Seir Kieran after a replay with St Rynagh's.

The drawn game was a low-scoring affair, as was the case a lot of the time when we played St Rynagh's. Most of the scores were from frees, and scores were hard come by. Conditions wouldn't have been great, but there was a huge crowd that time as well. Offaly were All-Ireland champions too, so there was that extra bit of interest in the county final.

It was one of those days where I knew I was striking the ball well and once the first free went over, the confidence was up.

It came down to the last puck of the game. The ball went out over the end-line. Martin Hanamy touched it and it was a '65'. Martin Walsh was the referee and he handed me the ball and told me it was the last puck of the game.

I put it down.

I hadn't missed a free all day. It sailed over the bar and we got the draw out of it. I remember the feeling of satisfaction, just knowing that we had one puck of a ball to decide if we were in or out of the championship.

We went on to win the replay, but knowing that when you were needed for your club, you delivered. That mattered hugely to me. I would put it down as the most important free I ever took.

Most of our team, including myself, would have been 10 years on the go... and then you had Joe and a few more who were 15 years on the scene. Our team was coming to an end. 1998 was a bonus.

JOE DOOLEY
(KEVIN KINAHAN)

OFFALY 0-16 CLARE 0-13
Semple Stadium, Thurles
All Ireland SHC Semi-Final, Second Replay
AUGUST 28, 1998

Fourteen years after playing in the 1984 All-Ireland final, Joe Dooley brought the form of his life back to Semple Stadium when Offaly beat Clare at the third time of asking in the All-Ireland semi-final.

★ **OFFALY:** S Byrne; S Whelahan, K Kinahan, M Hanamy; B Whelahan (0-3), H Rigney, K Martin; Johnny Dooley (0-1), J Pilkington (0-1); M Duignan, J Errity (0-1), P Mulhare; B Dooley (0-1), J Troy (0-1), **Joe Dooley (0-5)**. Subs: G Hanniffy (0-3) for Mulhare; J Ryan for Troy; K Farrell for B Dooley.

★ **CLARE:** D Fitzgerald; B Quinn, B Lohan, F Lohan; L Doyle, S McMahon (0-1), A Daly (0-1); J Reddan (0-1), O Baker (0-1); J O'Connor (0-6), F Tuohy, A Markham; N Gilligan (0-1), G O'Loughlin, D Forde (0-2). Subs: F Hegarty for Tuohy; D Scanlan for G O'Loughlin; C Clancy for Scanlan.

THE ACTION

IT WAS THE saga that gripped a nation but, in the end, Offaly had the final say after they beat Clare by three points to set up an All-Ireland final clash with their fellow Leinster men, Kilkenny.

After three games and loads of controversy, it was fitting that a scorcher of a day in front of a packed Semple Stadium would be the setting to bring an end to the saga.

Stephen Byrne had the game of his life between the posts for Offaly, but it was a man in the winter of his career at the other end who did the damage as the ever-green Joe Dooley proved unmarkable – hitting five points from play.

By the seventh minute, Offaly had raced into a 0-4 to 0-0 lead, with Dooley striking over two, but the next five belonged to the Banner County who rattled off four of their own to draw level and eventually take the lead in the 18th minute.

Offaly went on to lead 0-9 to 0-6 at half-time with Johnny Pilkington, Billy Dooley, Gary Hanniffy, Brian Whelahan and Joe Errity all finding the target. But the winners knew there would be a Clare re-boot, so two early second-half points from brothers Dooley, Johnny and Joe, were vital in stretching that lead.

Stephen Byrne was called into action to deny Danny Scanlon and Alan Markham, while Clare did get it back to a two-point game with 12 minutes to go. Offaly, however, smelled blood. They reeled off four points on the trot from Joe Dooley, Hanniffy (two) and Brian Whelahan ('65') and they held an 0-16 to 1-10 cushion coming down the final straight.

Anthony Daly and Jamesie O'Connor (two frees) brought it back to a one-score game again, while Byrne again was called upon late on to deny Fergal Hegarty. It was an edge-of-the-seat end to a trilogy that won't be forgotten anytime soon in GAA circles.

★★★★★

"

1998, THINKING BACK on it, was a big year for us.

We had won the All-Ireland in 1994, and were beaten narrowly in the final in '95. We were going for back-to-back All-Irelands and we were within two minutes of retaining the cup. Clare beat us on the day and it was bitterly disappointing.

We lost to Wexford in a big Leinster final in 1996, and lost to them again the following year, so doubts were creeping in if we would ever win another All-Ireland. Winning is all about self-belief, and that was starting to erode.

Babs Keating came in, in 1998 and, I remember, we had a meeting in the County Arms in Birr. He brought us in and put us all at tables, and did a bit of brain-storming about what we needed… what was missing and all that.

Babs told us that we were going to be the best team in Ireland but, not alone that, we will look and be dressed like the best team in Ireland, and travel to loads of places when we win things.

He painted us a picture that he was thinking… BIG.

We started training in the hall in Shinrone in early January. Johnny Murray was doing the physical training with us under Babs. We started doing circuit training and it was torturous stuff. We weren't really used to it.

We moved on to Banagher to do the outdoor training where we would start off with a three-kilometre run and finish with one as well, along with a lot of other running in between. We had trained hard under Éamonn Cregan in a different way. This was slogging. We continued with that training in the spring and even up until the championship. We played Meath in the first round and while we got over them, we were sluggish.

We had Wexford then and, again, there was no *life to us.* We were fit but there was no life to us. I think we were doing too much hard running and not enough ball work.

We got over Wexford.

We kind of robbed them really. They led the whole way through the game, but Johnny got a goal with almost the last puck of the game.

I will never forget the Sunday before the Leinster final with Kilkenny. We were in O'Connor Park in Tullamore. The old grass bank was there at the time and Johnny Murray and Babs decided that we needed a blow-out. We must have run up that hill 40 or 50 times on the Sunday before the Leinster final.

Normally, it would be a full match for about 40 minutes and ease off then, and be fresh for the following Sunday but, this day, we finished off with sprints up and down the hill in O'Connor Park.

There was a bit of discontent there, not only amongst the players… but I would say with the selectors as well because we weren't doing enough ground hurling and ball work.

We were beaten in the Leinster final, but it was tight. I think it was 13 scores to 12… Kilkenny got two goals from 21-yard frees from DJ Carey. We lost, but it wasn't really a *disaster.*

After the match, Babs got surrounded by journalists and they started asking him questions. He was in a corner and he threw the blame on the team. That was the wrong thing to do at the time, particularly when not everybody was really happy with how the training was going.

Babs left then, and Michael Bond came in.

I will never forget the first night Michael Bond came in.

I would always be early for training and, next thing, Michael came into the dressing-room. He took off his coat and was hanging it up on the hook. I forget who was in the room with me, but I turned around and said, 'Is it any harm to ask you… who you are?'

'I'm your new trainer!' he said.

'Well, you better introduce yourself,' I replied.

'I'm Michael Bond… from Loughrea!' That was the first we heard of him. We never looked back and, from the minute he came in, he was a breath of fresh air and so positive. He built us all up and encouraged us.

We got back to the hurling we were good at. There was no fluency to our game before that. The minute he came in, the ball was being moved.

I was playing in the full-forward line and before Bond came in, the ball never came in and you would nearly want a tracksuit on you in there… but now, the ball was coming every two minutes and my tongue was hanging out.

Personally, I improved a tonne and whoever was marking me would have improved as well.

Michael Bond came over to me one night at training and said to me, 'You have a brilliant first touch'. I was a bit taken aback.

I knew I had, but no one had ever said that to me. I perked up after and he also told me before the three Clare games that if I wanted to make a move... 'Don't be waiting for me to tell you!' He told me that I knew better than anyone on the field if a switch would benefit someone around me... or me myself.

We beat Antrim by eight or nine points in the first qualifier game and we were starting to loosen out a bit.

Before that game, we played Kilkenny in a challenge game and my brother Johnny got a bad belt and fractured his cheek-bone. That was a disaster, because Johnny was our talisman and we wouldn't have a hope without him.

He missed the Antrim game but made it back for the first Clare game, when he had to wear a faceguard. They played him corner-forward but gave him a licence to go wherever he wanted. We didn't want him in a man-marking role because of his injury.

We should have won that first game. Clare got a free to draw it and I don't think anyone knows what it was for.

We had no fear of Clare.

The replay was two weeks later on a Saturday. Clare were ready for us the second day. They had a big lead at half-time. I remember the Tall Ships event was on in Dublin that day and the city centre was packed.

We only got to Croke Park a half-hour before the game.

Joe Errity and Billy Dooley came on at half-time, Johnny went out to midfield, Brian Whelahan went up to the forwards and Michael Duignan went back to the half-back line.

We clawed our way back into the game and it was back to three points, before Jimmy Cooney blew it up early.

The crowd came on the pitch. I think it was Paudge Mulhare who beckoned everyone to come out onto the pitch. Straightaway, I felt that the GAA were in a bit of a corner and were going to have to give us something.

When you have 15,000 people out on the pitch, you have a problem. Ger Loughnane admitted on TV straight after the game that the referee had made a mistake and that opened up avenues as well.

We went up and had a few pints in the free bar in Croke Park. We gladly made use of that. We had a meal in the Spa Hotel after that, along with a few more pints. There was a team meeting called then. A bit of a debate started as to whether we would train the next day or not.

Michael Bond threw it out to the floor. Johnny Pilkington said that he wouldn't be training unless he knew there was a match. A few more had their say, but it finished up with Billy saying that if training was called, he would be there.

The meeting broke up then, but early the following morning we got word that we were getting the replay... so we trained that Sunday evening.

We went down to Thurles on the Tuesday evening before the game, and Offaly were on cloud nine.

The supporters were part of the sit-in and they felt they had contributed to getting a replay. Everyone felt more involved.

We thrived off that, to be honest. Our team was getting much stronger as well.

All we did on that Tuesday in Thurles was a bit of shooting practice and some ground hurling and, I remember, I couldn't find a place on the field where I couldn't puck the ball over the bar. There are times in your life when everything feels right.

I had to nearly go to the corner flag to try and miss a point. I was even putting bends on the ball... like the professional golfers with their draws and fades.

That transferred to the game then and I scored five points. I actually don't think I hit a wide that day although a couple did drop short.

On the Saturday of the game we got the bus down, and I will never forget driving into the square in Thurles. It was a real warm day and the place was packed. All the Offaly supporters were banging the sides of the bus on the way to Hayes' Hotel.

We could hear the crowd outside all during the team meeting in the hotel and if you weren't in the zone, you would have been terrified.

There was some sort of a game on before ours and I remember watching a bit of it. When we were getting up to head into the dressing-room, the stewards, who would have been mainly Tipperary guys, were all wishing us good luck... which was strange, because normally they would be neutral. Everyone was rooting for Clare in 1995, but they were shouting for Offaly in '98.

My wife's mother Mary Moriarty is a Cork woman and she lived across the road from the Poor Clare nuns in Cork. There was a Sister there called Sister Paul and she used to write to my own wife Marie regularly.

She gave us an envelope with a load of miraculous medals and little pins, so I handed them out before the game in the dressing-room and all of the players took them and pinned them inside their togs.

Even Johnny Pilkington took it... and you would think Johnny wouldn't care about that sort of stuff, but he took it and pinned it inside his togs too. It just shows you what players will do. Everyone is religious to a certain degree but players will do anything to try and win a match. Any advantage you get, you will take it.

The game was tit-for-tat but once we got our noses in front just before half-time, we stayed a couple of points ahead.

The game was unbelievable. We were beating a Clare team, who were double Munster champions and were All-Ireland champions. It was a sweet one... and to beat the Munster champions down in Munster as well! It was new ground for Offaly in a lot of ways.

After the game, the excitement and euphoria set in. We came back to Birr and into Molloy's pub. Meeting my own father and mother there, it was just unreal.

On the day of the game, my parents were in a pub in Thurles and Bertie Ahern happened to be there as well. He was Taoiseach at the time and he came over and introduced himself to them, after someone had pointed out to him who they were.

Everybody that was anyone was at the game... and it was a game that I will never, ever forget.

Offaly sold more tickets for that game than any other. Christy Todd told me that we sold 15,000 tickets. For an All-Ireland final, you might sell five or six thousand and scour the country for the rest of them.

The atmosphere in Thurles was special and different. It was all building up with the sit-down protest in Croke Park the week before, and it was redemption for the All Ireland final in 1995 as well.

Thurles is special. Everyone is together before and after the game, and the turf is special as well.

I had played there in the 1984 All-Ireland final and, 14 years later, I was still playing there. I was 35 years old in 1998 but I was never as fit and never in as good form. I had been commuting up and down to Dublin, but I had stopped that and was working down the country.

That helped and I was really enjoying my hurling.

Winning that game was brilliant but it would have been all for nothing if we didn't go on and beat Kilkenny in the final.

We had beaten Wexford, who were the Leinster champions for the previous two years, and beaten Clare, who were Munster and All-Ireland champions... and now we were playing Kilkenny, who were Leinster champions, in the final.

We got there in the end thanks to a great team performance. The switch of Brian Whelahan and Michael Duignan was a big factor, but it was more than that, it was a super team performance.

After that then, we went back to the club. We played a load of games one after the other. We got to the county final and that ended in a draw. We beat St Rynagh's in the replay, and we finished off the year on a high.

Being All-Ireland champions and county champions in the same year... nothing gets better than that.

KEVIN KINAHAN

Kevin Kinahan beats Charlie Carter to the ball in the 1998 All-Ireland final, when his summer performances earned him a third All Star award.

"

THE TRAINING IN the Brothers field in Birr was fierce tough under Éamonn Cregan. The field would be a meadow of grass at the start of the night, but we would have it nearly ploughed up by the end.

We had two bad lights there and, by God, was it tough training. I remember, Cregan got us a psychologist one evening in the County Arms and I fell asleep at the back of the room. The boys made some laugh of me. You know when a lad is ranting and raving, some people love it… but each to their own, I suppose.

Babs Keating came in, in 1998, and Johnny Murray came with him as the physical trainer. We did some colossal training under him as well in Banagher. Only for him, I don't think we would have won anything that year.

We used to do all the hurling and physical training, and then when training was over we would have to do three rounds of the pitches in Banagher. Not just one of the pitches but three rounds of the three pitches together!

You had to beat your time every night from the previous training; you always had to knock off a few seconds. Jim Troy, John Troy and myself... we would always be paddy last. But Johnny was a great motivator for training.

Winter training is nearly gone, I would say at this stage... it's all gone into the gym. We would have done a very small bit of gym work over in Ferbane, but we did all our dirty work out on the field.

I think that stood to us. Lads are gone mental into the gym now, but a lot of them are very bulky and not as fast.

I used to do weights when I was younger with Brendan Abbott. He used to mix up a potion of three raw eggs and yogurt after training, but then they thought I was getting a bit too big. Derry O'Donovan was the physical trainer with Cregan at the time, and he told me to stop doing the weights because it was slowing me down. Muscle is heavier than fat.

The best game for me had to be the Clare game in Thurles in 1998. It was like an All-Ireland final.

Coming out of Croke Park after the second game with Clare, it was all up in the air. Michael Bond came down then and said there was a chance of a replay and to take it easy on the pints, as we could be playing again next weekend.

When we saw the people sitting on the pitch, we kind of knew there was going to be *something*. Jimmy Cooney made a genuine mistake and he put up his hand; the GAA had no choice but to have a replay. Clare people will say that we stole their All-Ireland but there were a few minutes left, plus stoppage time.

That day of the third game in Thurles I was marking Sparrow O'Loughlin for most of the game, but three or four different lads came in on me throughout... Cyril Lyons was one of them.

Stephen Byrne stopped some bullets that day. Joe Dooley had a stormer with five points from play, but we all hurled well as a unit. It was unusual to see the whole 15 players outstanding for the full game. We were on top the *whole* game.

We couldn't wait to get out of the dressing-room. We were that focused, we didn't even notice the crowd. Pure determination.

Once your head is right, you are off to a good start.

The more you think of it, sure you would end up going out and not hitting a ball. I was very relaxed but everyone is different and players have their own mentality. Johnny Pilkington would go off and have a cigarette... same with John Troy.

I stayed quiet and said nothing to anyone. I would just get my head focused and concentrate on doing my job for the team.

Everything went right for us that day.

The tension would make the hair stand on the back of your neck. But still, we had won nothing after it; it was only a semi-final.

Myself and Martin Hanamy were chatting after the game and we were saying we better go on and win the All-Ireland because we had nothing actually won. It felt like an All-Ireland with the hype and all around it, but there was no silverware.

It took us nearly an hour to get from Thurles back to Hayes' Hotel after the match. We had to get a Garda escort. You couldn't walk down the main street of Thurles with the crowd.

We sensed that we were going to beat them the third day. The Offaly supporters really got in behind us. That day in Thurles, such a crowd... but three-quarters of those were from Offaly, no question about that.

My father never went to the pub, but he was coming home from the match that day with my two brothers, John and Kieran, and they pulled into Brereton's pub on the way home and he drank two bottles of lemonade. He would never go to a pub after a match.

You could see the sheer delight on people's faces after beating Clare.

We didn't have to put our hand in the pocket that night anyway. Everyone thought we were heroes and that's what drove us on to go and win the All-Ireland.

We were in the same frame of mind for the final as we were for the Clare game – we knew we had to win it. Imagine Kilkenny beating us in the All-Ireland after all we went through... and us having nothing to show for it at the end!

Michael Bond brought us in after the match and told us we had nothing won. We knuckled down then and it was two weeks of hard, solid training.

Beating Kilkenny in the All-Ireland final topped off the whole lot. As Hubert Rigney said when he went up to get the cup, 'We came in the back door, but went out the front door!'

Beating Kilkenny in an All-Ireland, especially after they beat us in the Leinster final, it can't get much better.

I was marking DJ Carey, and Charlie Carter came in on me for a while as well. It is a great feeling but it's not a nice feeling when you lose one. Losing one is like a death... I hated losing.

1998 was my best year. We won the county title and I was captain. I got an All Star as well, so that really topped it off.

I remember having the Sean Robbins and Liam MacCarthy Cups in Clareen for a week and bringing them around to families for photographs. It was something that those people might not see again, those two cups together.

We beat St Rynagh's in the county final after a replay. The club championship started two weeks after winning the All-Ireland.

That was Clareen's last time to win the championship... and I was the last man to captain them.

I am quiet generally. A captain is a leader and lads should look up to the captain. I didn't want to do it. The manager came to my house three times, begging me.

Michael Duignan came up to me at the bar on the night of the All Stars and told me that I was after getting another All Star. I couldn't believe it, to be honest. No one was supposed to know until it was announced, but someone had told Duignan.

I was delighted. It was my third one to get... three in five years, not too bad.

I got one at corner-back in 1995, and Martin Hanamy often said to me that I got his All Star. They put me in corner-back even though I played full-back. Brian Lohan was there as well at full-back... both of us actually got nominated for Man of the Match after the 1995 All-Ireland final.

DJ Carey and Joe Deane were top class.

I had a lot of tussles with Joe Rabbitte as well from under-21 and senior. DJ and Joe were very fast, however, and I remember before the 1995 Leinster final Martin Hanamy warned me not to let DJ out of my sight.

I would have been pulling at his jersey and all that, and he turned around and asked me if I wanted to get into his pocket? That was some day as well; it is always a great day when you beat Kilkenny.

I had a few bad injuries too. I got a trial with the minors, but I broke two bones in my foot. I played with the under-21s alright. Joe Dooley was over Clareen at the time and Padraig Horan asked him had he anyone to send in from Clareen... and he sent me! We got to two All-Ireland finals, but it is the only All-Ireland that Offaly haven't won.

I got a bad belt in a county final in the mid-90s and I broke two ribs and got pneumonia. I was in hospital for two weeks, and it nearly took me six months to recover. I did nothing about it and left it too long. I thought I was having a heart attack in the bed at one stage with the chest pains. I went into Brendan Lee and he sent me straight to Tullamore. Doctor Taaffe was on duty that night and he told me that he couldn't see any of my ribs on the x-ray... I had let things go too far. He told me if I was a smaller man, I would be dead.

I retired in 2002.

Lads were getting too fast for me. Training was getting very physical and there was more training and less hurling.

It was a big shock to the system. It took me a while to get used to it, to be honest. I was back with the club full-time but I missed the county lads and missed the banter.

Mike McNamara tried to get me to come out of retirement, but I didn't. It is hard on a young family. I had two young kids at the time.

I would often meet my wife coming in the door and I would be going out, to go to training... and not back until near midnight.

MICHAEL DUIGNAN

OFFALY 2-16 KILKENNY 1-13
All Ireland SHC Final
Croke Park
SEPTEMBER 13, 1998

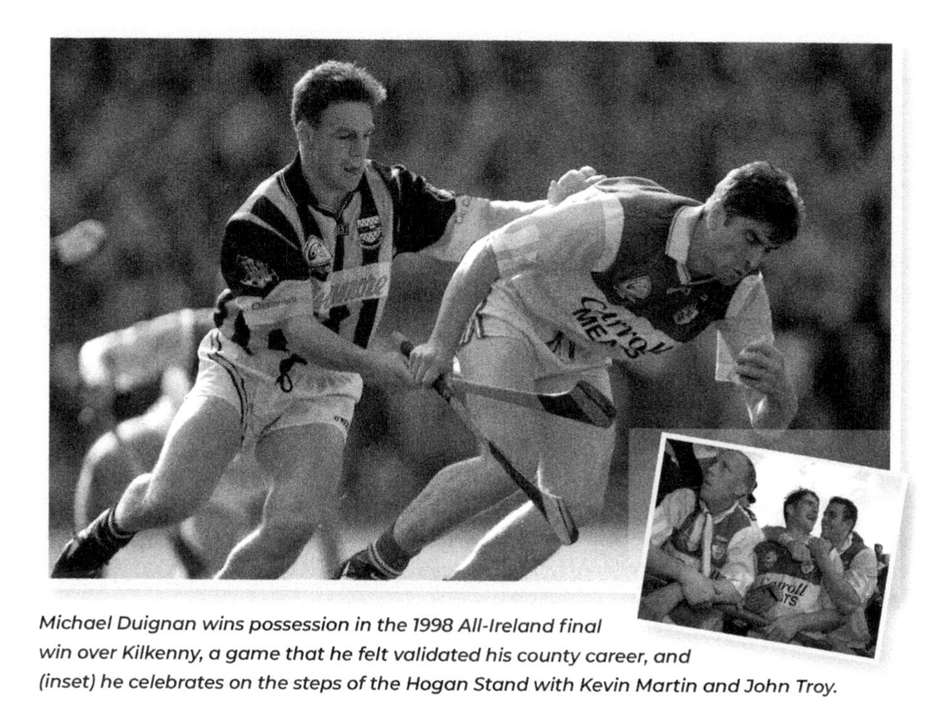

Michael Duignan wins possession in the 1998 All-Ireland final win over Kilkenny, a game that he felt validated his county career, and (inset) he celebrates on the steps of the Hogan Stand with Kevin Martin and John Troy.

★ **OFFALY:** S Byrne; S Whelahan, K Kinahan, M Hanamy; B Whelahan (1-6), H Rigney, K Martin; J Pilkington (0-1), Johnny Dooley; **M Duignan (0-2)**, J Troy (0-3), G Hanniffy; B Dooley, J Errity (1-2), Joe Dooley (0-2). Subs: P Mulhare for Hanniffy, D Hanniffy for B Dooley, J Ryan for Johnny Dooley.

★ **KILKENNY:** J Dermody; T Hickey, P O'Neill, W O'Connor; M Kavanagh, C Brennan, L Keoghan; P Larkin (0-1), P Barry; DJ Carey (0-5), A Comerford (0-1), B McEvoy (0-3); K O'Shea (0-2), PJ Delaney, C Carter (1-1). Subs: N Maloney for O'Shea, S Ryan for Comerford, J Costello for Kavanagh.

THE ACTION

OFFALY OUTSCORED KILKENNY 2-5 to 0-4 in the final 23 minutes of the All-Ireland final that brought an end to one of the wildest years in hurling history. Having come in through the back door, Offaly left through the front door as All-Ireland champions after reversing a Leinster final defeat to Kilkenny, dealing with a change of management, and the mental and physical fatigue that came after a pulsating semi-final trilogy with Clare.

Michael Bond, who took over from Babs Keating after that Leinster final defeat, had the Offaly men in tune as they finished strong, with Brian Whelahan running wild in the forward line having been switched from wing back in the opening half.

Truth knowing, Whelahan, who was suffering from illness, was struggling on Brian McEvoy but his switch up the field and Michael Duignan's move onto McEvoy worked a treat as Whelahan accounted for 1-6 of Offaly's 2-16 total. Midway through the first-half, with Kilkenny up by four points, Whelahan and Duignan made that game defining switch. Stephen Byrne made an outstanding save from Ken O'Shea eight minutes before half-time but late points from O'Shea and DJ Carey offered Kilkenny a 1-7 to 0-8 lead.

It was all-square at 0-12 to 1-9 with 48 minutes gone. The complexion of the game changed, however, a minute later when Joe Errity burrowed his way through the Kilkenny rearguard to hit the net.

Errity added a point and Offaly were in full flow. Carey blazed a penalty over the bar which was a massive fillip for the Faithful County, before further points from Birr comrades, Whelahan and Johnny Pilkington, put them four up with seven minutes to play.

Fittingly, the final two scores of the game fell to the two men whose switch shaped the game. Whelahan got in for a goal, after Errity did all the donkey work, before Duignan jumped for joy in the final minute with a magnificent long range score.

★★★★★

"

I PICKED THE 1998 All-Ireland final for two reasons.

One, because we beat Kilkenny in an All-Ireland final, and I think that game is often forgotten about in a way given the year that it was with the games against Clare and the whole Babs Keating affair.

Looking back on it now, it was a massive achievement in its own right. Personally, I often feel it was a vindication of my career… or summed up my career. That's my second reason!

We won the All-Ireland minor title in September 1986 and myself and Daithí Regan came straight onto the senior panel a few weeks later. It was a long journey until 1998… it was 12 years.

I actually missed the 1987 championship. Myself and Daithí went off to America for the summer. That's something I don't regret. It was great craic and a great experience. We spent 15 or 16 weeks over there and won the North American Championship.

I came home on a Friday, then played a county semi-final with my club that weekend and won my first senior county title a few weeks later… so 1987 was a great year, even though I missed out with Offaly.

I felt that if I didn't go then, I would never go because I had huge interest in hurling for Offaly. The following year, in 1988, we won Leinster and I moved to Dublin. For the next 10 years it became my life. I was training three or four times a week. In the early stages, I was single and we won three Leinster titles in-a-row and were beaten in three All-Ireland semi-finals.

There was a mixture of the young and old there, and we were sort of saying, 'Look, our day will come'.

We won the league in 1991 with a very young team, but were beaten in the first round of the championship in '92 and '93 by Kilkenny, who went on to win the All-Ireland both years.

All of sudden then, you find yourself at 26 years of age and your career is slipping… the All-Ireland medal hasn't arrived. We were very determined at that stage and we had the right age profile. We won the All-Ireland then in 1994.

I was obviously delighted and thrilled to get that All Ireland medal, but I got injured in the Leinster final that year, early on in the game. I tore ankle ligaments, but I played the whole game.

I knew from early on I was in big trouble but we were trying to win a Leinster for the first time since 1990, and there was fierce competition in the panel, so you just had to play through it.

I couldn't train up until the All-Ireland semi-final and lost my place as a result. I came on for 10 or 15 minutes at the end of the semi-final.

I often think about it.

I had three chances to score points when I came on in that semi-final.

I had two easy ones... hit one short and one wide, and I hit the hardest chance over the bar. If I had got the three of them, regardless of the injury, I would have had to start the final but I ended up aggravating the injury and wasn't picked to start.

I came on in the final and we won it. I made a positive contribution but there was something lingering with me after that.

Maybe there was an element of my own preparation, or lack of it. I was always very fit and played a lot of other sports to a reasonably high level. I always prided myself on my fitness and athleticism, but in those early-90s there was still a fair bit socialising going on and bits and pieces.

I think after the 1994 All-Ireland, I moved to another level in terms of my preparation and injury prevention. I used to get a lot of private physio that I would have paid for myself because I felt I needed it, and I never missed another championship match after that until I retired.

After 1994, my aim – morning, noon and night – was to win another All-Ireland with Offaly. It was all I thought about, and I had a lot going on. I was progressing in my job, got married in 1995, and bought my first house in Naas.

Moving to Naas... meant a lot of travelling.

The 1995 final didn't go well for us. We came back in 1996 and were very determined, but were beaten by Wexford in the Leinster final. They won the All-Ireland that year and they beat us the following year in Leinster again.

So now, another four years had slipped by, and we were after having a few different managers as well.

Babs Keating came in in 1998 and that's where the whole story on '98 begins.

Babs was in and Johnny Murray was with him as the physical trainer and he deserves huge credit for what he did. He was an army man and the work we did with him was incredible.

We needed a motivation as the team had a lot of hurling done. There was big mileage on the clock... and 11 or 12 of the team were on the go for a long time.

Gary Hanniffy and Ger Oakley came through in 1997 and made their debuts, but the likes of Simon and Barry Whelahan, Colm Cassidy and Darren Hanniffy and a lot of young blood came through then... and the young blood brought a buzz to it. It brought life into the dressing-room.

I think in terms of hard running, we probably trained way harder than teams do now. There was an issue then that this type of training was continuing on into the summer when, traditionally, we would do all hurling with maybe a bit of physical running at the end.

But we were still doing hill-running and a lot of physical work. Our performances in the championship were a bit lax but, looking back on it, the loss to Kilkenny in the Leinster final was six or seven points. There was nothing shameful about it.

But the fall-out started then, and Babs had a go at us.

I was probably not as aware of all that was going on in the camp because I used to travel to training with Babs. I would meet him in The Curragh and travel down with him.

We would have had woeful craic in the car. He was a great character and he was very good for me. He gave me great confidence that I was a crucial part of the team. Whether he was bull-shitting me or not, I don't know.

I was playing rugby that year as well. I played with Buccaneers in 1997 and we won the All-Ireland League Division Three title during that winter ...and I went back to it in 1998 and played with Naas. I was living there for a few years at this stage and they were onto me to play with them. We won the Towns Cup in 1998.

I was nearly training every night, either with Offaly or with the rugby, and come April and May I was in ferocious shape. So I was shielded a bit from it, but in hindsight and from talking to the lads after, they weren't happy with the training... and the fact that we were slowing down the ball and it was more about holding onto possession.

When the fall-out happened, it happened fairly drastically and quickly. So, all of a sudden… Babs is gone, we lost the Leinster final and we have no manager!

The back door was in, so we were still in the championship but it was very difficult to see where we were going at this stage.

Michael Bond was brought in and that proved to be a masterstroke. My God, the enthusiasm! I think if you had spent a year looking for the right person at that time, you wouldn't have found him.

We didn't need a big name; we had experience and leaders in the dressing-room.

The first night he landed in, he told us we had the best players in Ireland, we were the best team in Ireland and that we were going to win the All-Ireland. We were looking at him thinking, *Is this lad for real?*

We trained every second night from then on. It was all enjoyable and it was all ball-work. Our necks were on the line, and we often played our best hurling when we were in that situation.

Our first match was a challenge against Kilkenny, for an opening of a pitch or something. I didn't play because I broke a finger and I didn't even go to it. Johnny Dooley ends up breaking his jaw, so if things weren't bad enough, now one of our best players was out.

We went on and we got back on the bike. The three games against Clare were unbelievable. We got to the final anyway and it was my belief that we couldn't lose. The bond between the players and supporters was unbelievable.

The training session before we played Clare in Thurles… there were thousands at it. I remember coming through the open tunnel at the top of O'Connor Park and they all descended. I put up my fist at them, and the reaction was unreal.

We were to the pin of our collar, but we were there and I just knew that there was no way we were going to lose. The morning of the All-Ireland we arrive in the Spa Hotel… and Brian Whelahan is there, paler than a radiator.

He was the man for the big day.

The one thing you were guaranteed in a final, whether club or county, Brian Whelahan was going to be Man of the Match or very close to it… and now he was sick. I do slag him and ask him where did the 'flu go in the second-half, but he definitely wasn't one hundred percent.

I ended up being switched back, with Brian moving up to the forwards, but he wasn't doing that bad in the backs. Brian McEvoy got away from him for a couple of points but he also got away from me for a couple as well, and that is forgotten.

McEvoy was on fire that day... and Brian Whelahan actually cleared a ball off the line from PJ Delaney.

Stephen Byrne was cool and calm in the goals. Simon Whelahan was a forward with Birr but was corner-back and totally subdued Charlie Carter. Carter got a goal early on but, after that, he had the better of him.

Kevin Kinahan was immense and Martin Hanamy was like me, coming to an end and had huge drive. Hubie Rigney was forceful and Kevin Martin was unbelievable that day.

Johnny Pilkington and Johnny Dooley were in the middle of the field, and their natural game would be to drive forward and attack, but the way they worked in the middle and the physicality they brought was amazing.

Up front, it was tough going... but some of the artistry up there, particularly when Whelahan moved up there was magic.

The point in the first-half when Sid (Brian Whelahan) made the side-step and slipped the hand-pass to John Troy! Troy had the ball in the wrong hand, switched hands and put it over. If you watch the way he did it...

The short line-ball from Whelahan too! Joe Dooley was on the go the guts of 20 years and he got some brilliant points.

Joe Errity was probably the most under-rated or under-stated hurler on the team. He had horrific cruciate injuries in the early-90s and was a massive full-back and centre-back for Birr. For him to go and do a job in the forwards then... I was thrilled for him. He scored 1-2 in that final.

I have talked about Michael Bond, but he had the likes of Paudge Mulhare and Pat McLoughney with him. Pat isn't with us anymore, unfortunately. Tony Murphy, the hurling secretary as well! They lived for Offaly hurling.

Pat McLoughney said in a video one time that he used to be up in the fields on his own just thinking about Offaly hurling and, as time goes on, you realise how important those men were.

Our chairman at the time, Brendan Ward, had a big call to make with Babs as well. Christy Todd was a very good secretary. Things were being done right. You were looked after and there was never a question of anything not being done.

Things went well for me in the final. One of the things I would have struggled with in my career was the belief that I was good enough at that level.

I played a lot of sports but I would have had a doubt in my mind when looking at the really top players. I knew I wasn't as good as them, but you have to realise and say, 'What can I do *for* them?'

In 1998 I was corner-forward, wing forward, midfield and wing back. It didn't matter, and off the field I would have been one of the more experienced players as well.

When I reflect back now, I think it was a vindication of all the years and all the travelling. It was never a sacrifice. I would be getting out of bed at 6am. I had a fairly responsible job and I needed to get my work done. I wouldn't get home until midnight on training nights but I loved it, and I always looked forward to it whether it was winter or summer.

My son Sean was born in February of 1998 as well... there was a lot happening. It was a real happy time at home. God rest Edel, at the time there was never a question. It didn't matter how often I had to go training or whatever, we always worked it out. She had a busy job in Dublin at the time as well.

For a lot of reasons, it was a special year for me personally and for the team. The final was also a brilliant game of hurling and it was down to the wire, but having that feeling with three or four minutes to go that you weren't going to be beaten was special.

We knew Kilkenny were *gone.*

KEVIN MARTIN
(SHANE DOOLEY)

TULLAMORE 2-12 KILCORMAC/KILLOUGHEY 0-11
Offaly SHC Final
O'Connor Park Tullamore
OCTOBER 18, 2009

Kevin Martin turns away after scoring Tullamore's first goal in their historic county final win in 2009 and (inset) celebrates with his son Oran after the victory.

★ **TULLAMORE:** D Fox; A Martin, C Bane, S Egan; N Mannion, B Dagg, H Treacy; J Keane, S Kelly (0-1); E Finnerty (0-1), J Duffy (0-1), G Treacy (1-0); **S Dooley (0-7)**, **K Martin (1-1)**, F Kerrigan (0-1). Subs: S Martin for Finnerty, P Kelly for Mannion.

★ **KILCORMAC/KILLOUGHEY:** S McDonald; J Grogan, D Kilmartin, C Guinan; C Cassidy, P Healion, K Leonard; C Mahon, E Lee; B Leonard (0-4), D Currams (0-1), M Leonard (0-3); C Slevin (0-2), G Healion, J Gorman (0-1). Subs: P Cummins for Gorman, K Grogan for Slevin, D Kilmartin for M Leonard, J Wynne for G Healion.

THE ACTION

HISTORY WAS MADE in O'Connor Park as a bumper crowd of over 9,000 lay witness to Tullamore claim their first Offaly senior hurling title since 1964.

Having almost exited the championship at the group stage after losing their opening five games, Tullamore roared into life in the knockouts – taking out St Rynagh's and Birr en route to putting hot favourites Kilcormac/Killoughey to the sword.

Despite Shane Dooley missing two penalties, the Tullamore men still had five points to spare in the end as they enhanced their reputation for performing on the big days. There were jubilant scenes after the game as Tullamore finally got over the line, with player/manager Kevin Martin in the thick of it having won his first senior county medal after 19 years in the jersey.

Martin proved a handful at the edge of the square in the first-half in particular. There as a target man, he won clean and dirty ball, while his size and strength earned him a penalty even if Dooley failed to convert. Coming near the end of the opening half, Dooley's effort for a score was scuffed but it came into the path of Martin, who found the net to give his side a 1-6 to 0-5 half-time lead.

Kilcormac/Killoughey worked hard in the second-half and did get it back to a one-point game before a fortunate Ger Treacy goal from 40 metres once again put Tullamore in the ascendency to lead 2-6 to 0-8. The outsiders never looked like buckling after that and outscored their opponents 0-4 to 0-1 from the 40th to the 46th minutes to pull away in style, with Dooley landing two fantastic scores, while Jody Duffy and Shane Kelly also got their names up in lights.

★★★★★

"

I WAS THE only man on that Offaly panel when we were winning All Irelands that had no club senior medal. Everyone else had county medals.

It was 1964 since Tullamore won a senior hurling title and I was 19 years trying myself. There was 9,000 officially at that match but there was probably 11,000 there; some of them haven't been seen since and won't be seen for a while.

I came in as manager in 2008. We were beaten in a quarter-final by Kilcormac/ Killoughey down in Banagher. They beat us by 10 points, and they probably could have beaten us by 20 points. That was our seventh weekend on the trot between hurling and football.

That year in June, we played the Galway under-21s in O'Connor Park, and that's when we peaked. Anthony Cunningham was managing Galway and we beat them by seven or eight points.

We were flying it. And we said, 'Right this is the year'... and that was it, that's when we peaked, it was downhill after that, but anyway, that's going off track.

Definitely that final, for me, because we were written-off. I couldn't understand that because Tullamore are always good in finals. Nine times out of 10, we are good in finals. Of course, we brought in paper clippings into the boys of interviews from Kilcormac and I remember one of the Healions, I think it was Ger was doing an interview... and he said, 'If we don't get complacent, we should win it,'... this sort of stuff.

Listen, we used every little thing to fuel the fire. The footballers were beaten early that season and the thing just took off for us then. We had a full run of seven or eight weeks where it was hurling only.

We won the semi-final by two points against Birr. I was never in a dressing-room as good as that Tullamore dressing-room. There were some characters in it, like.

I remember actually the Sunday morning of the final, I went to mass... and Jody Duffy was sitting maybe four or five seats across from me and I'd say it was his first time in mass in about 10 years.

I'd say the souls of his shoes were melting. We had a woeful sneer over that, so when Duffy was at mass we said, *That's it, we are going to win it.* The whole build-up was massive because the town had not been in one for so many years.

I suppose to actually win it with the lads you grew up with, the lads you went to school with, lads that you soldiered with for so many years... the likes of Damien Fox. Alo and The Gift (Damien Fox) were selectors... and PJ, my brother, was involved. I had hurled with them for years and it was just mad... that definitely had to be the game for me.

We celebrated for about a week afterwards, it was brilliant.

I was manager and playing so that's when I thought, *Right, I'll pick that game because it was special for me.* Having said that, it was easy enough to manage them. When they saw what sort of a panel we had, everyone bought into it then... it was magical.

We used to go up to the pool in the Tullamore Court Hotel after training and even Alo Lawlor used to get in. Alo would be sitting in the jacuzzi and there'd be steam coming out of him... and Shane Kelly would be over picking out his hair. It was woeful craic.

While the lads would have been really nervous, I wasn't because I was after playing with Offaly in front of thousands. And while it was my first club hurling final, a good few of us had played in football finals, so I was relaxed enough.

We were lucky enough on the day as well because I got a goal in the first-half after Shane Dooley mishit a shot. He was going for a score and it came in low and I just added to it, and it went into the net. So, we had some rub of the green, even though I won two penalties and Dooley missed the two of them!

I should have taken the second one... but anyway!

I remember Eddie Finnerty jumping over whoever was wing back, maybe Colm Cassidy? Eddie grabbing a ball and popping it onto Jody Duffy... and Jody down the wing and over the bar, just little things stick in your head. Eddie would be small and wouldn't be renowned for catching the ball over anyone's head.

We played St Rynagh's in the quarter-final and they were nine points up, I think, at half-time, and I came in as a sub then. I got a goal and Shaun Martin got a goal... and Francie Kerrigan actually got five points from play that day.

He stepped up and we beat them by a point or two. That was the start of it. It got rolling after that. That was the first time we beat Rynagh's since... God knows when! We didn't even look like we were going to come out of the group or qualify at all before that game.

But that was the thing with the dual player. There's football, hurling... football, hurling. It was great when the football finished. We had maybe eight or nine dual players. It goes to show when you're not hurling all the time, you won't be at your best.

Starting out the year, I was always going to play some part. I actually remember the semi-final, a windy day against Birr in O'Connor Park. I said to the boys 'Listen, if we are playing against the breeze in the first-half, I won't start!'

I was down to start, but I said, 'I won't start. I'll come in at half-time when we have the breeze'. My legs were nearly gone at that stage, so it was just to hang in around the square.

We ended up playing with the wind in the first-half and I ended up staying on for the whole game. It wasn't one of my better games, but that's the way I was thinking... I was trying to use whatever strengths we had.

We probably only had 18 or 19 players that you could call on. Shaun Martin was on the bench, Pe Kelly was on the bench... maybe another one or two, but after that, it was young lads. So, we were very lucky with injuries. But I was always going to play *some* part.

When we got to the 2009 final, one lad in Digans pub said, 'Now, you don't play a starting role in the final... you'll be a better impact sub'.

I looked at him and said, 'I am starting in the final and that's it... I've waited 19 years!' I have to say, we had a bit of luck in fairness, but when we clicked and things started to roll, we were good enough.

We always knew it was going to be next to impossible to keep a lid on the build-up to the final. People know me, I don't like all of the hype around finals and lads talking in the papers and TV interviews and whatever. I try and keep it as low key as possible, but we are in a town and it was always going to be next to impossible.

In fairness to the lads, we kept our feet on the ground and we had loads of meetings after training... and we talked to them all the time. The Gift, Alo and Christy Geoghegan were very good for that. They are all lads that are experienced at the top. It wasn't just my voice all of the time.

It was electric around the place, absolutely electric. It was brilliant. It's back in 2009, but it's only like five years ago with me. And it's the same with Damien...

The Gift had been there for so many years and he was 46 or 47 years of age playing a county final in goals. It just meant a lot to everyone, and the club.

After the final whistle went it was just elation. I'll never forget it.

I fell to my knees. I shook hands with Healion... and the first fella that ran into me was Donie Beatty.

He flattened me onto the ground. I'll never forget it. Of course, I was sweating, muck to the gills... and people just coming up... hugging us. It was like winning the All-Ireland for us. I was delighted for the young lads. The likes of Brian Hogan, Declan Hogan and all those boys were only chaps at the time, and it just meant so much.

Even Stephen McDermott, who used to look after the grass in O'Brien Park! He used to go around in the tractor cutting the grass. Stephen was sick at the time; he had cancer and was dying. He came over with his wife after and he was crying.

He shook my hand and that meant a lot. It was the same with Tommy Kelly, Peter's father. It just meant so much to those types of people. It was unreal.

It was surreal to win, because we were 7/1 in a two-horse race.

Alo actually said it to me, 'Say nothing to the boys!' And we collected a fiver off every player... and we put it on.

After the game, there was a big cheer in the dressing-room. I gave a bit of a speech and told the lads we had a few pounds to collect. We had €3,500 or whatever it was to collect, and the place went mental.

I didn't tell them I had us backed; we said we'd just do it for the craic.

The amount of old people that day on the pitch, just to see their faces! While it was elation for me, I had won All-Irelands and everything else... but it was the other people, the coaches when we were younger, those types of people were there, and it will stay with me forever.

It's hard to compare it to the All-Irelands... county is different.

When you wait for so long and when you are 19 years playing before you get one, it's just *different*.

It was earned. And then we got a bye in Leinster, beat Clonkill in a semi-final and played Ballyhale in the final. The lads got a chance to play against Henry Shefflin, TJ Reid... it was memorable stuff for them.

The town was buzzing, like for a week after that. We were out every day for a week. The Bridge House gave us a dinner one of the nights and we were in a few different places around town getting fed. They all wanted a piece of it. When I think of it… if I could do it again!

It was like a wedding that went on for a week.

I managed the playing and managing well.

Believe it or not, when you're playing, you can actually see things that lads can't see from the line. I remember on the day, Nigel Mannion had an outstanding game. But for the last 10 minutes, his legs were gone. I can't remember who was on him, but they went forward with a ball with about 10 minutes to go and Nigel was getting it hard to catch up.

I shouted over to Alo and told him to get Nigel out of there… and get Shaun Martin in wing forward. From time-to-time, you would see things that lads wouldn't be watching on the line.

I could see it from an end-view camera or whatever, so it was good that way. I could talk to the lads too. When you are shouting in from the sideline, it's different, but when you're in the middle of them, you can point and you can make sure that they're playing when they're supposed to be playing… or taking up the shape they're supposed to be taking. It's very beneficial actually, being a manager and playing.

I started on young Damien Kilmartin. I caught a couple of balls off him and they brought in one of the Healions and sure it was always going to be a tussle after that. I knew that I would be a handful for him anyway without being electrifying, but all I was there for was to hold the ball up, catch a few balls and throw it around.

It wasn't as if I had blistering pace or anything.

In fairness to Shane Dooley, even though he missed the two penalties, he still knocked over three great long-range points in the second-half and they were killer scores that would suck the life out of any team… so he made up for it in fairness to him. He was capable of doing everything.

He was coming into his prime at that age. He was a serious bit of stuff. And he was a serious free-taker, and when you have a really good free-taker, and he's a really good player, that's a bonus.

He kept us in a lot of games, in fairness. But that's what he was there for. As Roy Keane would say, 'That's his job'.

Stephen Egan was corner-back; he was brilliant, a class act. Stephen would make any team on his day. Excellent hurler, loads of pace, brilliant at reading the game. Absolutely guaranteed Man of the Match, hands down... brilliant, and that would be nine times out of 10.

Benny Dagg was centre-back. Benny did a lot of blocking and a lot of work that went unseen. You don't have a team like that and not have a good centre-back. Benny was under-rated. He was an excellent player. An excellent centre-back and he showed it then in the Leinster final on Henry Shefflin.

I think Shefflin got one or two points max, and that was it. Benny's in America now, in California or San Francisco; he's married out there and, to be honest with you, we never really replaced him. He was there the next year in the final and I think he went the year after, in 2011. We never actually filled that position.

If I was never to manage a team or never to play again after that match, I wouldn't have cared... that was *the* match.

I'm gone from management now due to family commitments.

I always say family comes first, livelihood comes second... and then it is your sport, if you're serious about it. So, I had to stick by my word. Whether I manage again in the future, I don't know... that's for another day.

SHANE DOOLEY

Shane Dooley lifts the trophy after Tullamore's historic county final victory in 2009 (inset) and in action for Offaly in the Leinster Championship earlier that season.

"

WE PLAYED BALLYSKENAGH towards the end of the group stages, and it was a kind of a relegation final... without the official title of it. We beat them that day in Kinnitty and that put us through to a quarter-final. But it's amazing the way the whole season just took off after that.

The year itself was the same as any other really. Kevin took us over and he was very organised. Training was going very well but, I suppose, the group was a disaster the way it worked out for us... until the last game.

We were being well beaten by St Rynagh's in the quarter-final and I don't even know where the belief came from at half-time in that game, but we said we would come out and get the win out of it.

I'm not sure what we were down... maybe 10 or 11 points, but to come back and win that game, maybe that's where it all started. The belief came that we could mix it with the top teams then.

St Rynagh's are a good hurling team and when they're going well, their hurling is slick. I think we just came out in the second-half and got stuck into them. We just clawed it back and maybe there was a bit of a 'smash and grab' at the end.

If there was Hawk-Eye that day, you wouldn't know what way it would have gone when Francie Kerrigan scored a point at the end. I'll give him the benefit of the doubt and say it was a great score, but it could have gone either way.

In 2007, I think we beat Kilcormac/Killoughey in the championship and it was a comfortable enough win in Tullamore. The following year, they beat us in the quarter-final, so it was our second time getting to the knockout stages with that team.

Then going into the semi-final, we played Birr. We had played Birr at the start of that year too. They had just lost the All-Ireland final to Portumna and I think we might have been their first game back in the first round.

The way we won that game! There was just this level of confidence there and, in fairness, at training every night everyone knuckled down... we were professional in our approach.

During the Birr game then, we just mixed it with them from start to finish, and we got in front near the end then and just pushed on. It was a huge performance. They got a goal near the end through Stephen Browne, and we still went on and got the next two points to win it.

It was a huge deal for us... like, that Birr team were going for five in-a-row, and to have won those two games coming into the final, it gave us serious self-belief.

You could see before the final that lads were focused, and it was like that for every game... quarter-final, semi-final and the final, just the level of focus from everyone was unreal. It was unreal to go from one end of the scale to the other.

Looking back at that team, one of the things that stood to us, and you can see it in the final... you can even see it in the Leinster final when we got that far was the great level of fitness in the team. Lads worked hard and, I suppose, the hurling just clicked then from the quarter-final onwards.

Kilcormac/Killoughey were being talked up that they were going to have a handy final, because it was us that was in it. And people nearly had us beaten out of it that day.

I can't even imagine what sort of mental journey they went through coming up to the game… and maybe the nerves of the actual final and the crowd stunned them a little bit. Then when we came out, you could see in lads' faces… the focus. The nerves and the chemistry were just perfect for a good performance on the day from us.

From the very start of the match, we just took off like; it was 'helter-skelter' right from the throw-in. No one had time to even look up and pick out a pass. It was just launch it as far as you could! And there was a lot of breaking ball.

It's amazing how hurling has changed over the last few years… like, that doesn't happen anymore.

We got a point, but we went down then. They scored a couple and we went behind… and we drew level, and we went behind again. We went behind a couple of times, but we didn't cave, we kept plugging away.

I missed a penalty then, and it still haunts me. But even when that happened, they went down and got a free, but they missed the free… it could have been a four-point swing! And they got the next point, so it could have been a five-point swing in the space of a minute… but we stayed going.

The second penalty I missed didn't really matter, to be honest. The game was won at that stage… we were seven points up, I think, with something like five minutes to go.

The two penalties still haunt me to this day.

I was lucky enough there wasn't a whole lot riding on the second one, but the first one was the *one*! What I miss in a match is what kills me and I missed two '65s' and two penalties that day. I could have had 2-9 in a senior hurling final… it would have been a sweet one to be able to say, but in fairness Kilcormac/Killoughey missed a right few that day too.

I changed my hurl for the second penalty.

The hurl I was using that day, I had it pieced and it just broke… and had just cracked a little bit before the game. This hurl was part of my arm at this stage so I said, *I'm not changing it.* I noticed hitting penalties before that the piece must have been giving way every time I hit the ball at my hardest, and the ball wasn't going as fast as I would have liked... so that's why I swapped the hurl for the penalty and ended up missing it.

I made a show of myself that day for the penalty. Keith Begley came in with a spare hurl and Colm Cassidy made a big deal about it when they stopped him coming in, so I was putting more pressure on myself.

Ger Treacy hooked three lads with his body that day... the level of commitment from everybody was savage. Lads were throwing their body in the way... the hooks, the blocks. Every one of our lads in defence got the better of their man that day.

Midfield was huge. James Keane had an outrageous performance and Shane Kelly hurled fierce well too, but Keane popped up everywhere in the second-half clearing balls. Between himself and Stephen Egan, you would nearly think there was nobody else in our back-line.

We got some good scores at the other end too, though we probably got lucky with the two goals... and the way we got them. But we still missed two penalties, so things evened out in the end.

Over the whole course of the game, we never really felt like we were going to lose it and with 10 minutes to go, the game was more or less over. You could see the life was gone out of them, and they were bringing off lads and bringing on lads. They were expecting to win, and things went so bad for them and went so well for us... it knocked the life out of them a small bit.

We still would have been talking ourselves up.

They might have beaten us the year before, and I think Brian Leonard scored six or seven points from play the year before. But the year before that, we beat them... so we knew it was in us to beat them, if we hurled well on the day.

Of course, Kevin Martin would have been drawn on the underdogs thing and no one giving us a chance... our backs-to-the-wall, that type of thing! But still, he would play to our strengths as well. He wouldn't have been one to dwell too much on other teams and I think between himself and Damien Fox, they were very good at talking to us.

Talking up our own strengths and giving us belief in ourselves rather than looking for inspiration elsewhere.

We had Kevin at one end of the field, Damien Fox at the other... and then we had PJ Martin, Christy Geoghegan and Alo Lawlor on the line. We had Pe Kelly on the line too... we had experienced lads on the line who could see the way things were happening.

If the game was running differently, it would have been a harder game to manage from the line, but I think the game managed itself. There wasn't any need for switches. Every lad was hurling well... if there were a few lads being skint, it might have been a different story.

Damien Fox had a fantastic game in goals and made numerous good saves, while Kevin got a goal and a point from play and won two penalties but, realistically, he could have won five or six if the referee was giving us what he should have given us.

You couldn't say we would have been better off with the two boys on the line making switches or anything.

We'd have been winning games before where we thought we had it won, and then we'd be beaten at the death, so I just remember trying to work my backside off and try and get back into defence, and help, just to make sure nothing went wrong in the last few minutes.

It was savage but, in fairness, all the lads stayed in the present and just kept playing ball, kept hurling away and no one gave up until the whistle at the end.

When the final whistle went, it was surreal at the time. The crowd that day, I have never seen it at a county final... like, you would hardly see it at a county match. They said there was 9,000 at it but if you look back, the stand was full and the terrace was three-quarters full.

The pitch was just packed when the whistle was blown, and the crowd came in.

I don't know how long it took us to get to the stand but it really hit home when we got up there... went up the steps and had a look down. The crowd there was just phenomenal. It was unbelievable. I remember looking out across the crowd... and not being able to believe it.

I was just gone 23 at the time. I was 16 playing senior hurling for Tullamore, so I had been hurling six or seven years at that stage. I didn't feel young being captain.

We had a young team. The majority of our team was that age... 23 or 24, with a couple of older lads, but it was a good blend and I suppose it just mixed well on the day. I knew Kevin would cause hassle in the full-forward line. Jody Duffy was one of the older lads at centre-forward, but never stopped going all day, worked hard and got a couple of points.

Benny Dagg at centre-back let nothing by him all day; he was like a brick wall there.

Kevin Martin is a good man to hurl beside, because there was nobody going to win a ball off him too handy in the air. We knew the ball was going to break around him. When he got it, he'd throw it out. But myself and Francie Kerrigan… it was kind of one going behind him and one go in front of him, and hoping for the best.

If you take me out of it, Francie and Kevin are going to take watching from any defence. So it did take the pressure off me in the full-forward line and it worked well. We had three different styles of hurlers in the full-forward line, and we all did our bit on the day.

There are video clips taken from the day of men who aren't with us anymore, and it's great to be able to look back at that and see the joy on their faces. It's something people don't think of doing… going into a dressing-room with a camera and interviewing lads, and just catching that raw emotion after winning a game.

You get away from the crowd… and in with each other. The dressing-room was brilliant craic.

The only thing I found hard to do was to sit down the day before, thinking if we win… thinking of some sort of a speech. I thought I was jinxing myself sitting down to write some Irish the night before, but I tried to do it as quickly as possible and forget about it until after.

Kevin had us fairly well focused. No one was to do interviews; no one was to talk to papers. We were coming in under the radar and we were going to keep it that way. 'Keep the heads down and don't be putting unnecessary pressure on yourself by talking to the papers,' he told us. Everyone followed that plan, I thought.

Sunday morning came. I sat down to read the *Sunday Independent* and here was this two-page spread on Damien Fox in the middle of the paper. In fairness, he hurled well that day but I thought it was funny. Only he would have gotten away with that.

”

RORY HANNIFFY

BIRR 2-5 YOUNG IRELANDS 1-2
Leinster Club SHC Final
O'Moore Park, Portlaoise
DECEMBER 1, 2002

Man of the Match Rory Hanniffy (right) and his brother Gary, who captained Birr to a Leinster final win over Young Irelands in 2002.

★ **BIRR:** B Mullins; G Cahill, J Errity, JP O'Meara; N Claffey, Brian Whelahan, D Franks; J Pilkington, Barry Whelahan (0-1); D Pilkington, G Hanniffy, **R Hanniffy (1-2)**; P Molloy, S Browne, S Whelahan (1-2). Sub: L Power for Browne.

★ **YOUNG IRELANDS:** M Carey; C Carroll, E Farrell, C Fitzgerald; S Byrne, T Drennan, C Phelan; J McDermott, O Carter; J Fitzgerald, J Carey, C Carter (0-1); D Carroll (1-0), DJ Carey (0-1), D Carter. Subs: P O'Neill for D Carter.

THE ACTION

REIGNING ALL-IRELAND CLUB champions Birr were forced to muster up every morsel of their steely determination to see off Young Irelands of Kilkenny to retain their Leinster crown for a record -equalling sixth time.

It wasn't a game for the ages or the purists, but rather one where the team that dug the deepest would come out on top. Rory Hanniffy was the main man for Birr. He went between defence and attack and in the end hit a sizeable 1-2. Indeed, he scored as much on his own as the entire Young Irelands' team.

In atrocious weather conditions, and with a brave 8,000-strong crowd in attendance, Young Irelands opted to play against the wind and up until close to half-time, their plan worked a treat. Their teak tough defence was holding firm, but it was in their star-studded forward line that they struggled.

After Simon Whelahan opened the scoring for Birr, Dick Carroll hit the net for the Kilkenny men after six minutes to give them a shock lead. Barry Whelahan landed an elegant point to cut the arrears to one before a final 10-minute surge at the end of the half sent Birr in leading at half-time. Rory Hanniffy pointed nine minutes before the break, and five minutes later he hit the net with a ground shot from about 25 metres. Simon Whelahan also pointed a free to give Birr a 1-4 to 1-0 lead at the break having played with the wind.

Tempers flared at the start of the second-half, before Charlie Carter clipped over the opening point on 39 minutes. Once again, it was Hanniffy who replied with his second point of the day on 41 minutes. The remaining 19 minutes of hurling saw both packs of warriors only manage one score each.

The Birr offering was a second goal three minutes from time, with Simon Whelahan firing home after good work from Paul Molloy.

★★★★★

"

I AM TERRIBLE at remembering any sort of match I played in. I actually met Paul Cleary recently and he laughed at the idea of me having to remember and talk about a game.

I was tossing around the idea of going with the Leinster minor hurling final that we won with Offaly in 2000 but, for me, looking back, the most enjoyable games were Leinster club games with Birr.

The games were generally rough and ready, and there was never anything between the teams. I suppose my fondness of the Leinster club games stems from the fact that I actually made my senior debut for Birr in the Leinster Club Championship.

When I came onto the scene in 1999, I didn't play in the Offaly championship. I wasn't even on the panel for the county final, but ended up starting the first round of the Leinster club. We did win an intermediate title in Offaly that year and I was on that team before making the step up to the seniors after the county final.

I remember going down to the match. It was against Kiltegan, down in Aughrim, and I brought my own jersey because I was sure there wouldn't be enough of them to go around by the time they got to me.

Around halfway through the journey down, our manager Pat Joe Whelahan told me he was going to start me... and there was no one more surprised than me.

Fast-forward three years to 2002, and I'm now established on the team. I actually managed to get a look at the game recently and I can tell you there were more mistakes than anything else. But to me, I think it summed us up at that stage.

We were known as a skilful team but it didn't matter how skilful we were that day, it was all about rolling up your sleeves to go out and win it.

We were All-Ireland champions going into the game and one of the reasons I picked this game was we were playing against a team with DJ Carey and Charlie Carter in it. I actually marked DJ for a period and that kind of gave me a thrill, even in the heat of battle.

It was a supreme team performance. DJ only got a point from a free and Charlie only got the one point as well.

Personally, I always got the most enjoyment out of those types of games. It was the kind of game where one hook could have been the difference between winning and losing.

Even to this day, if you ask anyone about that game, the weather will be mentioned. It was absolutely cataclysmic. There was hardly a blade of grass left on the field after the game.

I remember family members from Dublin, who used to come to the games, and meeting them after. They were soaked and could barely walk across the field.

Birr had never lost to a Kilkenny team and I don't think Pat Joe had ever lost to a Kilkenny team either. While we were taking on the likes of DJ, Charlie Carter and Pat O'Neill, we always felt we could win the match.

The club season could start in February and not end until the following March, with games in all types of weather, and we had done that for a few years, but in typical Pat Joe fashion, he had us just right.

After a Leinster Championship, we generally lost that fitness over the Christmas and had to suffer again in January... but the fitness of the guys that day was savage considering the conditions.

I came onto the Offaly team in 2001 and we were well beaten... and the same the following year. The pattern was starting to show that we were not going to be able to compete with Kilkenny, but for the next few years we could very much compete as Birr.

The one thing I do remember about the game was that we had a meeting the night before in Dooly's Hotel. I actually used to enjoy those meetings but on this particular night I was in the middle of exams and I fell asleep during the meeting.

I went on to play relatively well the next day despite being so tired and what not, but it goes to show you, sometimes preparation doesn't really matter... things either just work out or they don't.

Having watched the game back, the one thing I noticed was that Brian Whelahan was hurling a different game to the rest of us. He was moving at a different pace; he was unbelievable. His frees were absolutely shocking though and I am looking forward to reminding him of that the next time I see him.

Barry Whelahan's work-rate and engine were unreal. He was hooking and blocking constantly over the 60 minutes. Joe Errity and Gary Cahill in the backline were getting away with murder.

The score was 2-5 to 1-2, so there isn't a whole lot to say about the scoring. In ways, it was comical to look back on the match. There were 21-yard frees being missed and lads taking shots where the hurl was going further than the ball.

They led for a period in the first-half, but only by a point, and there was never any panic stations. Simon Whelahan and Brian missed frees and, in general, we missed a good bit from open play too.

The match is summed up by the second-half. We were playing into a gale and it had to be ground out. We soaked up the pressure but made hard work of getting any scores.

We beat Ballyboden in a Leinster final a couple of years later, but a lot of the lads had moved on by then. I was now one of the more experienced lads on the team at that stage but looking back on it, playing with those lads in the Leinster club final in 2002... that was *the* thrill.

I count myself very fortunate to have played with those men and the most significant part of my playing days was getting to play with them rather than anything I did myself. On and off the field, it was great. They lived life to a different beat and still managed to be hugely successful while doing things their own way.

I got Man of Match as well, which was a very rare occurrence. I didn't remember that I scored 1-2, to be honest. I read back on the match report from the local paper a while ago and I have to say that Alan Walsh, who was the reporter on the day, was extremely kind with the description of the goal.

It was as much a mishit as anything else. The goalie was probably unsighted and it certainly wasn't a pile-driver.

I couldn't speak highly enough of Pat Joe Whelahan.

Firstly, he was the man who gave me my break and, when you go on and win a few All-Irelands with the same manager, you will always have a connection with him.

I just loved hurling while he was there and I can't pay him a higher compliment than that. I was in college in Galway and I lived for driving home twice a week to train. I had a non-existent college life really and I don't regret it in the slightest.

He had the philosophy that if you were faster than everyone else, then you would get the ball… and if you had the ball, then you were in control. It was stamina training by virtue of repetitive speed training.

Johnny Pilkington used to joke that you would be hearing the start of the *Coronation Street* music going to training and hearing the end of it on the way home. Training was short, but it was so intense.

We would train on the hill in the Community School and there would be food for us in the County Arms, but I left training so many nights thinking I wasn't going to be able to eat. You would eventually come around a bit and get some food, before the drive back down to Galway.

I was fast, so I liked that training. Plenty of people have said to me that anyone could have trained that team but that couldn't be further from the truth. To train a team that used to have to play 12 months of the year in all different conditions and scenarios! Then you have all the dynamics of fallings-in and fallings-out that go with any team.

He would have tailored his training too. The older fellas would have got a bit of leeway at times but he knew how to get a performance out of us.

I remember we played Glenmore in a Leinster club game one year and he told us to target their corner-back. We were told that every time he got the ball to overpower him with numbers.

I doubt he sat down and watched videos of this guy, but he knew something anyway because the amount of ball we turned over off him was unreal. It was simple things. If he thought a keeper was a bit windy, he wouldn't be shy about telling you to run him into the back of the net on the first high ball.

We all made our debuts very young and he wasn't afraid to throw us in.

It was about winning, of course, but we just had great fun in the process. The buses home from the matches were just the best of craic as well. I remember after one of the All-Ireland finals, Midlands 103 radio got on the bus with us and my brother, who plays the harmonica, along with a couple of singers were all singing… and the whole thing went out live on the radio.

MICHAELA MORKAN

OFFALY 2-12 WEXFORD 2-10
All Ireland Intermediate Camogie Final
Croke Park
SEPTEMBER 12, 2010

Michaela Morkan holds aloft the Jack McGrath Cup after Offaly defeated Wexford in the All-Ireland Intermediate Camogie final in 2010.

★ **OFFALY:** A Kennedy; F Stephens, L Keena, K Brady; S Sullivan, **M Morkan**, L Sullivan; A Watkins (0-1), M Crean; J Brady (0-2), A Kelly, S Flannery (0-4); K Nugent, E Dermody (2-3), T Hannon. Subs: M Davis for Kelly, A Hughes (0-1) for Nugent, E Dunne (0-1) for Flannery.

★ **WEXFORD:** H Jacob; J Hayden, L O'Leary, C Atkinson; F Doran, L Codd, Shelley Kehoe; E Moran, L O'Connor; F Rochford (2-1), S Nolan, S Redmond (0-1); Stacey Kehoe, Ciara O'Connor (0-5), Lisa Bolger (0-2). Subs: B Curran for Doran, S Sinnott for Moran, Linda Bolger (0-1) for Stacey Kehoe.

THE ACTION

TWELVE MONTHS AFTER winning the All-Ireland Junior Camogie crown, Offaly were crowned All-Ireland Intermediate champions after seeing off a fancied Wexford side in Croke Park to make the step up to the senior ranks in 2011.

Joachim Kelly's troops made it an historic double at headquarters. They held off a brave fight-back from the Wexford girls, but Offaly had the foundations and held on to secure the win.

Elaine Dermody was the hero of the hour with a personal haul of 2-3, with her two goals in the opening half really creating a buffer for the Offaly girls to build on. At the other end of the field, it was a case of an old head on young shoulders as centre-back and captain Michaela Morkan produced an exhibition of hurling, giving her the unique accolade of not only captaining her team to glory but also picking up the Player of the Match award.

Offaly got the dream start and raced into a 1-5 to 0-0 lead. Dermody's first goal was an attempt for a point, but Wexford keeper Helena Jacob misjudged the delivery. A brace of points from Dermody and Jean Brady was added to by Siobhan Flannery, and Offaly were on their way. Wexford did manage to get a few scores on the board, but were hit by a second Dermody goal after she flicked to the net, while two more from the free-scoring Siobhan Flannery had them leading by nine points at half time – 2-7 to 0-4. Offaly looked destined for success but the second-half turned out to be a nervy affair.

Fiona Rochford goaled twice for the Wexford women in the third quarter and, suddenly, the sides were level with 11 minutes to go. Wexford outscored Offaly 2-4 to 0-1 in that period.

Offaly stayed calm and a beauty of a score from substitute Ailsa Hughes ended a 15-minute scoreless return, followed by a point from Siobhan Flannery. Wexford were staying in touch but late points from Emma Dunne and Arlene Watkins made sure that 20-year-old Michaela Morkan got to climb the steps of the Hogan Stand and collect the cup.

★★★★★

"

OUR WHOLE THREE-YEAR journey was unexpected, I guess.

It started in Mountbolus in 2008, that was Joachim Kelly's first session with us. I remember him taking us down to the corner of the field for a chat at the end of training and he said, 'Ye will be in Croke Park in September'.

We were looking at each other thinking, *He's gone mad, he doesn't realise!* I never thought I'd get to win an All-Ireland or play in Croke Park at all... and then we ended up there three years in-a-row.

That was the start of it. I suppose, Joachim put a spotlight on Offaly camogie at the time. He has a presence about him and instils a sense of belief into a team. We started to hurl well and celebrate the wins and the losses, and really bonded as a team. But still, in the back of my mind, I thought there was no way we were going to end up in Croke Park.

Eventually, we made it to the All-Ireland semi-final against Waterford in 2008. I can still remember the day, it was pouring rain and I was taking a free in the last few minutes and my hurl went flying out of my hands. We were up a good few points in the final stages of the match which meant we could enjoy the fact that we were into the All-Ireland. I'll never forget that day.

The management left no stone unturned in terms of preparation that year and the lead-up to the All-Ireland. They made sure we had a pitch to train on, got food after matches and had gear for the All-Ireland. I started playing for Offaly when I was 14 and since then, each year has been different... some years we'd hardly get a pair of socks, or we'd struggle to get a pitch to train on... and other years we would get soup and a sandwiches after training.

But Joachim made sure we were well prepared. We even took a trip to Croke Park on a Monday evening before the All-Ireland. We walked around the pitch and went into the dressing-rooms... I suppose to get rid of any nerves we might have had on the day.

The majority of the team had never played in Croke Park before so it was a great idea and a nice experience too. We stopped in a chipper on the way home – that wasn't ideal!

I was meant to start in college the week of the All-Ireland but I didn't go because I didn't want anything to interfere with the match. I was particular about things like that. If I hurled bad in a match I would convince myself it was the late night or one drink I had about three weeks before it. As the years went on, I was nearly worse... my friends used to go mad because I'd never be out. I'm a little bit more relaxed in recent years.

I remember the journey to Croke Park; I don't think I was too nervous, probably because we had made that journey up on the Monday evening. Catherine Byrne made a playlist for the bus. I still have the CD; we listened to that the whole way up and, as usual, I had a little power-nap.

We lost our first All-Ireland, the junior All-Ireland to Clare. We lost in the worst way too, with a goal in the last minute of the match. Shonagh Enright scored the goal; she started in NUIG the same year as me and they called her, 'Throw-na' because she actually threw the ball into the net... she would say that herself.

I think myself and Tina Hannon were in shock that day, because there wasn't a tear shed until we got to Kilcormac... and then we couldn't stop. It was obviously heart-breaking but the experience itself was unbelievable, even getting to play in Croke Park.

We knew we could do it then. Joachim was right all along, and going into 2009 we knew there was a strong possibility of wining the All-Ireland.

In 2009, we actually did it. We beat Waterford to win the junior All-Ireland, and it was unbelievable watching Marion Crean lift the cup. On the way home we stopped in the Spa Hotel, and Joachim put the cup in the middle of us all and we sang the *Offaly Rover*. We stopped in Tullamore, Kilcormac, Rath and Birr.

We went to Shinrone on the Monday night because Marion was captain; that was very special for us. The amount of people that came out to support us in every club, it was unexpected to be honest. We made the most of the winter; we probably visited each club with the cup more than once.

We gave ourselves two years to win the intermediate All-Ireland. I remember training in Birr Community School, down on the all-weather pitch and Joachim and Ger Fogarty called me over to tell me they were making me captain for 2010. I couldn't believe it to be honest, I was only 20 at the time.

I was still very quiet and I remember them telling me I didn't have to change anything; I could do my talking on the pitch... and that made me feel a bit better. I was so happy to be captain but still worried that I wasn't going to be good enough or do enough to deserve the captaincy. But we had so many leaders on the team at the time, like Marion Crean and Elaine Dermody... I could list off so many, so thankfully I was able to hurl away and let the girls do the talking.

Little did I know I was going to get to lift the cup that September. That year we lost to Wexford in the league final and in the first round of the championship, and then we had to play them in the All-Ireland. It was probably a blessing that they had beaten us twice.

I can't remember much in the lead-up to the actual match. Joachim wouldn't have done anything major. Just a quick chat between ourselves... he wouldn't have changed anything.

I remember a few things from the day itself. We didn't have a great start to the day. Joachim was lying on the back seat of the bus sick, and he was in and out to the toilet the whole way to Dublin. We were very relaxed going to Croke Park this time round.

We followed a Garda escort to the stadium and, just before we arrived, myself and Marion were feeling hungry so we got a couple of breakfast rolls.

Nutrition wasn't as important as it is now... and we won, so it obviously didn't do us any harm. I remember the dressing-room, going off to the little warm-up room on my own for a few pucks. I also remember the warm-up... my legs felt very heavy, I felt tired and drained. I talked to myself and told myself, *This is okay.*

I turned it around, telling myself, *I'm getting this feeling out of the way before the match starts.*

That was great, because since then, anytime I feel tired or my touch is bad, I think, *This is brilliant, I'll be flying it for the match.* That was probably the best thing that ever happened me. It's all a mental thing for me, and it's amazing how you can turn it around so quickly.

At half-time in the match, Joachim put a photo of the 2008 All-Ireland and '09 All-Ireland on the wall and asked us how we wanted to feel at the end of the match? I thought that was a nice way to motivate us, make us remember the feeling we had when we lost in 2008.

The match itself, I think we were up nine points at one stage and then they came back to level with us in the last 10 minutes. Only for Elaine Dermody... she had 2-3 scored at that stage! Emma Dunne and Ailsa Hughes came on and got a point each, and Arlene Watkins got another point to finish it. We won by two in the end. We've had many battles with Wexford since.

There was a little bit of panic at the final whistle. I thought, *Oh God, I am going to have to make a lot of speeches.* But I enjoyed it; I didn't let it take over.

We celebrated for months, and there was talk of us going skiing. We actually had a meeting and everything in the County Arms but we had a couple of girls who were underage so we didn't get to go.

I was only 18 when we got to the first All-Ireland. I don't know if that was a good thing or a bad thing, because I kind of took it all for granted. I'm 31 now and I haven't got to play in Croke Park since I was 20. But still, I'm so happy and glad for all those great memories... it was such a special time and I'm glad I got to be part of it all.

Audrey Kennedy was in goals and she would have been one of the more experienced players at the time. There was a nice mix. Shelia Sullivan, Marion Crean, Elaine Dermody and Audrey were in the All-Ireland against Tipperary in the early 2000s. They were well beaten, but they still had that experience of playing in Croke Park.

The management team were all very different people, with different strengths. They were a good team. Joachim just has a presence, and he obviously had a belief in us. Now, if you look at the team on paper, there was so much talent. You had girls who wouldn't miss training... you would *never* miss training.

You wouldn't want to let the management down, that's how much respect we had for them. You wanted to be at every training night because it was enjoyable as well.

We were winning so much at that time and we were loving it. You were just enjoying it so much, that it was easy to go to training.

Training was tough, of course. We used to play 70-minute matches in the Community School during the summer. There was nothing better! Joachim would be roaring in at us telling us to be more ruthless. I think he even pulled a hamstring himself one evening, marking Mark Corrigan.

He loved bad weather too, so he could run us. It was more of a mental thing than anything. I remember the dirty nights running up and down the field in Crinkle and Rath. And they're the nights you cherish... when you are in the last few minutes of an All-Ireland final.

BRIAN CARROLL

COOLDERRY 1-15 OULART THE BALLAGH 1-11
Leinster Club SHC Final
Nowlan Park, Kilkenny
NOVEMBER 27, 2011

Brian Carroll does a publicity shot during Coolderry's historic run through the Leinster and All-Ireland Club Championship in 2012.

★ **COOLDERRY:** S Corcoran; B Kelly, T Corcoran, A Corcoran; K Brady, J Brady, B O'Meara; K Teehan, D King; **B Carroll (0-3)**, B Teehan (0-1), C Parlon (1-3); E Ryan (0-1), M Corcoran, D Murray (0-6). Subs: K Connolly (0-1) for M Corcoran, S Connolly for Kelly, M Bergin for K. Brady.

★ **OULART THE BALLAGH:** B O'Connor; P Roche (1-0), K Rossiter, B Kehoe; S Murphy, D. Stamp, L Prendergast; M Jacob, D Redmond; D Nolan (0-2), G Sinnott, E Moore (0-4); R Jacob (0-1), F Cullen, N Kirwan (0-3). Subs: S Doyle (0-1) for Moore, D Mythen for R Jacob, P Murphy for Cullen; A Kavanagh for Nolan.

THE ACTION

COOLDERRY CLAIMED THE Leinster club title amidst glorious scenes in Nowlan Park, as the underdogs came and conquered. Wexford kingpins Oulart The Ballagh were the fancy coming into the game, but Coolderry put in a massive display steeped in heart and determination to reach the Promised Land.

While they were ravenous, there was no shortage of class about them either. Cathal Parlon fired 1-3 – a serious return considering he was being marshalled by Keith Rossiter – while the cool and calm free-taking of Damien Murray didn't come as a surprise to anyone who has seen the pocket rocket in action before.

Having failed to score in their county final success or in the Leinster semi-final victory against Ballyboden, Coolderry talisman Brian Carroll opened the scoring with only seconds on the clock to set the tone for his day.

Oulart came back strongly and led 0-3 to 0-1, but Ken Hogan's Coolderry were made of stern stuff and hit a purple patch to pull ahead. Scores were swapped coming up to half-time as Coolderry went in leading, 0-6 to 0-5. After the restart, the Offaly men kicked for home. A Parlon goal sparked them into life. Despite being bottled up, he made room and raised a green flag.

Coolderry kept the pressure on with four of the next five scores, the last of those an inspirational effort from that man Carroll. Oulart refused to go away, but could only match Coolderry score for score rather than close the gap. The Offaly men led by seven points coming into the last 10 minutes, but the Wexford champions saw a glimmer of light when corner-back Paul Roche drove a close range free to the net.

There would be no further scores in the game, as Oulart proved wasteful and really should have had themselves in a position to make it a nervous finish for new kings of Leinster, Coolderry.

★★★★★

"

AFTER 2010, WE felt we had a lot to prove the following year. People were almost saying that we won a soft county final in 2010, but you forget that Tullamore beat St Rynagh's, Birr and Kilcormac/Killoughey on route to winning their title in '09, so they were a serious team and they gave us a right battle in 2010.

In 2011, we had matured as a group. Ken Hogan was over us and he had us primed to win another county final and maybe do ourselves justice in Leinster, because back in 2010 we took a lot of abuse over losing to Raharney.

A lot of that came from 'hurlers on the ditch', but it did seep through to our mindsets.

We had to win the county final the hard way in 2011. We beat Clareen by three points, scoring three on the bounce at the end to win it. We played Kilcormac in the semi-final. They had our number in knockout hurling at that time so beating them was a big monkey off our backs.

We were back into the final then against our old enemy Birr. Whatever it is about us in finals, we seem to start really well. We hurled great in the first-half, but Birr came back into it very well and it was real cagey going down the final straight.

That kind of set us up and we now had won back-to-back titles in Offaly but, amazingly, for all Ken Hogan had won, he told us in the dressing-room after that it was the first time that he had retained a county title as a manager.

We went off then and trained extremely hard. We played one challenge match against Carrigtwohill, who were the Cork champions. We murdered them by about 20 points and we thought to ourselves that we were going okay, but we were also thinking maybe that they weren't great.

Their manager came in after and told us that they were after playing a lot of teams in challenge matches, but that we were the best team that they had played by a distance.

I think that might have planted a seed in our heads.

Ken had us well primed for the Leinster semi-final against Ballyboden. We had never played them in championship before, but we had hurled them in challenge matches over the years and there was a bit of needle there.

They had a couple of imports with them, along with Conal Keaney, Paul Ryan and the likes. We weren't expected to get anything out of that game but I remember Ken told us that we were going to be like the Japanese in Pearl Harbour – we were going to fly in under the radar and we were going to drop the bombs.

That's exactly what we did. They left us waiting too. They came late and the game didn't start on time. It was bully-boy tactics, but we were ready for them. It was a real team effort. Cathal Parlon and Eoin Ryan had great games. The Coolderry supporters were unbelievable as well and it was huge to get over the line.

It was a whirlwind couple of weeks... and now we had a Leinster final ahead. I actually don't remember the two-week lead up to the game.

The only thing I remember was the training on the Wednesday before the game. At this stage, I had gone two games without scoring. I didn't score in the county final or in the win over Ballyboden.

I was playing a different type of role... I was dropping deep a good bit. It wasn't an instruction from the management, but it was just natural to provide cover for the midfield and the half-back line, while making space for Eoin Ryan, Cathal Parlon and Damien Murray.

I was under a lot of personal pressure going into the Leinster final. The lads were jeering me over not scoring and they probably thought that I didn't mind it and I could brush it off, but inside, I was eaten up and it bothered me that I wasn't even scoring a point.

At training on the Wednesday, I couldn't hit the ball more than 30 yards. I was missing left and right, and only scored about one shot out of eight. I was putting myself under pressure more than I needed too.

We used to drive to matches and we always went in the same cars. Barry Teehan used to drive and he would bring myself, Paddy Teehan and Kevin Teehan. It didn't matter where the game was, that was the car load.

Earlier that morning, I went to my dad's grave just for a bit of solace. You're just looking to be the best that you can be and for that extra bit of energy.

We got to O'Loughlin's GAA club before the match and we had a cup of tea. I remember seeing David King, who was only 18, coming in with pasta and chicken in a plastic dish. I knew he was doing the right thing, but he was only 18... and so strong willed and professional... and that stood out to me.

We were quietly confident. We were in a good place.

We played into the wind in the first-half. Oulart had lost the 2010 Leinster final so they were in their second Leinster final in as many years.

They had so many household names; they had 11 starters that were on the Wexford team at the time.

If it was a year previous, I don't think we would have stood a chance.

The first-half was tight and cagey. I was worried about not scoring but, 10 seconds into the game, I got a chance and nailed it. I remember going, *Yes, I am in this now.*

We led at half-time 0-6 to 0-5. I think Oulart had eight wides in the first-half and they would have been disappointed having played with the wind in the first 30 minutes. They had a half-goal chance in the first couple of minutes but after that, midway through the half, I broke onto a puck-out and gave it to Eoin Ryan and he was unlucky not to get a goal.

We were up for the battle but we were playing a lot of aimless hurling, especially hitting long balls into our forward line.

Cathal Parlon and Keith Rossiter were having a serious battle on the edge of the square. Rossiter had come out with some ball, but Parlon got two points off him in that first-half.

Kevin Brady was tremendous also. He never gave Mick Jacob a sniff of it for the whole 60 minutes and he ran himself into the ground. He had to go off with cramp eventually in the last minute. They had to drag him off.

Trevor Corcoran was super at full-back and Alan Corcoran was having a massive battle with Rory Jacob.

Joe Brady was colossal at centre-back. The last thing you do with Joe is put ball down on top of him… so he lorded it.

Kevin Teehan started quietly, but worked hard and came flying into it. Damien Murray was the same. He came out and roamed around to get into the game.

Half-time was very calm, no roaring or shouting.

I have been in dressing-rooms before where we would be roaring about what it means to us and all that, but it was a Leinster final, the biggest game in the history of the club... we all knew what it meant.

Our work rate was starting to wear down Oulart. They were being forced into poor shot selection. Doubt was creeping into their mindset.

Oulart were really slow coming out in the second-half. They left us waiting a few minutes, but we came into small groups and just turned it into a positive. They got back level straightaway, but that was to be the last time that they would be level.

We got a goal then. Barry Teehan made a superb block down, Eoin Ryan got onto the ball but lost it, before Cathal Parlon got it.

It was surreal.

Everyone just seemed to just stop, Cathal included.

There was a hurl between his legs and Keith Rossiter was hanging out of him. Everyone was waiting for the referee to blow, for either a free out or a free in, but no one seemed to know what was going on. Cathal took off again... straight for goals.

He went for it and found the back of the net.

We forced that goal with our work-rate. Within a few minutes, we tagged on a few points and we were now five up, 1-8 to 0-6.

Oulart came back into it; they got a few scores and brought it back to three points. We turned it on for a few minutes again before Cathal Parlon had a goal disallowed.

That didn't rattle us. Straightaway, Damien Murray scored a delightful point from play and I got one of my most memorable points ever shortly after. From under the old stand in Nowlan Park, I fired over from 70 yards.

We were lucky to have the likes of Kevin Connolly to come on. He was on the team in 2010, but he got injured and Ken made the decision not to rush him back and used him from the bench. He slotted a lovely score from 30 yards.

We went seven points up with 10 minutes to go, and we thought we were cruising. We gave away a soft 21-yard free and Paul Roche nailed it to the bottom corner. He drove it low which was clever because that was the place to put it when facing Joe Brady on the line.

We slag Joe about not getting down quickly enough and it is nice to have been able to have a laugh about it and bring him back down to earth, because he got the official Man of the Match award on the day.

We forced them to hit more wides... it was great testament to our defence. We all funnelled back and worked as a unit as we knew Oulart needed a goal.

They had a late '65' after Stephen Corcoran made a great save from Nicky

Kirwan, but that trickled wide. Next thing we knew, James McGrath was calling for the ball and the game was over.

It is hard to put into words. It is something like I have never experienced on a hurling field and I have had some great days on it. That sheer excitement... it was almost overwhelming. It was a real let yourself go moment.

The supports flocked onto the field and it was a really special couple of minutes.

We were lucky to win a lot as a group, but this was beyond our wildest dreams... to have that with your friends that you grew up with!

It was very poignant that Mick Murray was a selector with us because he was the one that started us all off when we were nine and 10 years old. He instilled the core values and ideals of playing for Coolderry.

Hurling is a way of life in Coolderry. We don't have anything else in the parish. We have no pub and no shop. We have the church, the national school, the hall... and two hurling fields.

I remember being on such a high for days.

You didn't need drink. I didn't have a drink that night until about 10pm. I didn't want drink to cloud that feeling.

Seeing my mother and wife Aisling after the game... they are the ones who know what you are going through. I had put my best foot forward and got on the score-sheet while working hard for the team.

We were very conscious of respecting what we had done. We were going to celebrate but we were going to celebrate the *right* way.

In the backdrop of all this, my granny was 91 years of age and starting to fail. She was following all my games really closely. After the county final, I went straight to my auntie's house in Clareen to see my granny with the Sean Robbins Cup.

After the Ballyboden game, I rang her and the same after the Leinster final... I rang her because it wasn't possible to go see her. I had arranged to go see her in the days after, but I got a call to come quickly as she was failing.

She passed on, but that Offaly and Leinster campaign really kept her going, listening in on the radio. She took great pride in us winning those titles. She was president of the club.

She was buried the week after the Leinster final. It was the same weekend as

Kevin Brady's stag in Lahinch.

They went down, but they all got on a bus the next morning and the 30 or so of them were back for the funeral and did a guard of honour. It showed the respect we had for each other and what hurling meant to us.

The easy thing for them to do would have been to stay in bed in Lahinch, but they all got up and came back. They did the right thing as Coolderry hurlers.

You are like brothers on the field. That is one of the things that Mick Murray impressed on us.

The wake for the funeral... there were hundreds there.

It was quite funny, looking back on it. Most people were like, 'Sorry for your troubles but that was some win the other day!'

It was typical rural Ireland... and my granny would have loved that.

MORE

GREAT

SPORTS BOOKS

FROM

HEROBOOKS

TIPPERARY

GAME OF MY LIFE

THE GREATEST TIPPERARY hurlers over the last 50 years remember the one game in blue and gold that defined their lives...

Including: Jimmy Finn, Theo English, Tony Wall, Tadhg O'Connor, Dinny Ryan, Babs Keating, John Sheedy, Ken Hogan, Colm Bonnar, Cormac Bonnar, Declan Carr, Michael Cleary, Pat Fox, Conal Bonnar, Declan Ryan, Michael Ryan, Joe Hayes, Eamonn Corcoran, Tommy Dunne, Shane McGrath, James Woodlock, Brendan Cummins, Eoin Kelly, Michael Cahill, Brendan Maher, James Barry, Seamus Callinan and more...

A game that will live with each person forever.

Author: Stephen Gleeson
Hardback: €25.00
Paperback: €20.00
Ebook: €9.99
ISBN: 9781910827185

Buy on **Amazon**
(and paperback available in all good bookstores)

GALWAY

GAME OF MY LIFE

TWENTY-FIVE OF GALWAY'S greatest hurlers remember the one game that will live with them forever...

Including: Jimmy Hegarty, Ned Dervan, Andy Fenton, Iggy Clarke, Sean Silke, Joe Connolly, PJ Molloy, Noel Lane, John Connolly, Mike Conneely, Anthony Cunningham, Pete Finnerty, Eanna Ryan, Gerry McInerney, John Commins, Michael Coleman, Micheál Donoghue, Padraig Kelly, Kevin Broderick, Ger Farragher, David Collins, Ollie Canning, Alan Kerins, Fergal Moore and Gearoid McInerney.

A game that will live with each person forever.

Author: Ollie Turner

Hardback: €25.00

Paperback: €20.00

Ebook: €9.99

ISBN: 9781910827284

Buy on **Amazon**

(and paperback available in all good bookstores)

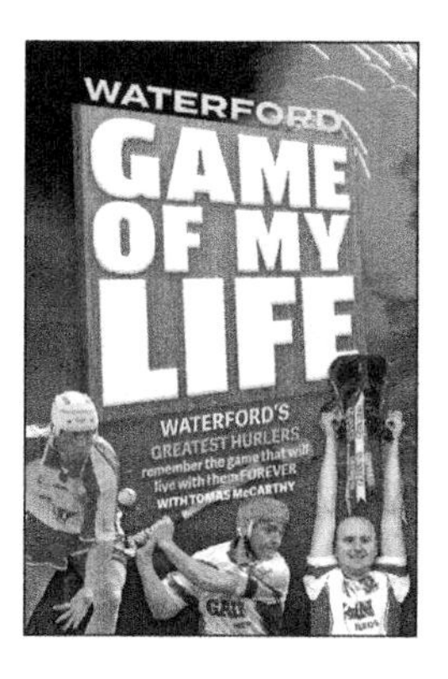

WATERFORD

GAME OF MY LIFE

25 OF THE GREATEST WATERFORD hurlers over the last 60 years remember the one game in their careers that defined their sporting lives.

Including: Tom Cunningham, Martin Óg Morrissey, Michael O'Connor, Larry Guinan, Jim Greene, Brian Greene, Patricia Jackman, Mossie Walsh, John Galvin, Shane Ahearne, Stephen Frampton, Fergal Hartley, Sean Cullinane, Brian Flannery, Eoin Murphy, John Mullane, Beth Carton , Paul Flynn , Dan Shanahan and Maurice Shanahan

A game that will live with each person forever.

Author: Tómas McCarthy
Hardback: €25.00
Paperback: €20.00
Ebook: €9.99
ISBN: 9781910827406

Buy on **Amazon**
(and paperback available in all good bookstores)

DUBLIN

GAME OF MY LIFE

25 OF THE GREATEST DUBLIN footballers over the last 60 years remember the one game in their careers that defined their sporting lives.

Including: Jim Crowley, Bernard Brogan Snr, Paddy Cullen, Tommy Drumm, Tommy Conroy, Gerry Hargan, Johnny Magee, Paddy Christie, Paul Curran, Vinnie Murphy, Kevin Nolan, Charlie Redmond, Paul Griffin, Ray Cosgrove, John O'Leary, Barney Rock, Kieran Duff, Jack Sheedy, Alan Larkin, Robbie Kelleher, Shane Ryan, Ger Brennan, Tommy Carr, Ciarán Whelan, Collie Moran and Alan Brogan

A game that will live with each person forever.

Author: David Sheehan
Hardback: €25.00
Paperback: €20.00
Ebook: €9.99
ISBN: 9781910827383

Buy on **Amazon**
(and paperback available in all good bookstores)

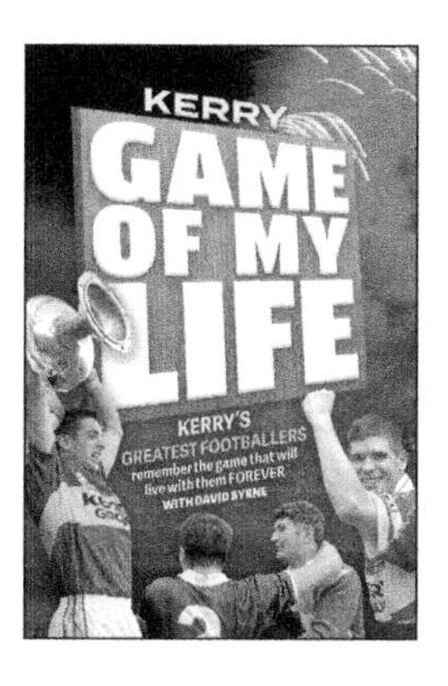

KERRY

GAME OF MY LIFE

30 OF THE GREATEST KERRY footballers over the last 60 years remember the one game in their careers that defined their sporting lives.

Including: Mick O'Dwyer, Sean Murphy, Michael Gleeson, Ger O'Keeffe, Ger Power, Mickey Ned O'Sullivan, John O'Keeffe, Paudie O'Mahoney, Sean Walsh, Eoin Liston, Mikey Sheehy, Jimmy Deenihan, Ambrose O'Donovan, Tommy Doyle, Jack O'Shea, Billy O'Shea, Dara O'Cinneide, Darragh O Se, Tomas O Se, Seamus Moynihan, Mike Frank Russell, Sean O'Sullivan, Eoin Brosnan, Marc O Se, Killian Young, Darran O'Sullivan, Tom O'Sullivan, Kieran Donaghy, Eamonn Fitzmaurice and Fionn Fitzgerald

A game that will live with each person forever.

Author: David Byrne
Hardback: €25.00
Paperback: €20.00
Ebook: €9.99
ISBN: 9781910827390

Buy on **Amazon**
(and paperback available in all good bookstores)

MEATH

GAME OF MY LIFE

25 OF THE GREATEST MEATH footballers over the last 60 years remember the one game in their careers that defined their sporting lives.

Including: Peter Darby, Jack Quinn, Mattie Kerrigan, Sean Boylan, Colm Coyle, Liam Hayes, Bob O'Malley David Beggy, Colm O'Rourke, Martin O'Connell, Bernard Flynn, Kevin Foley, Finian Murtagh, Tommy Dowd, Trevor Giles, Darren Fay, Graham Geraghty, Jody Devine, Ollie Murphy, Stephen Bray, Anthony Moyles, Kevin Reilly, Joe Sheridan, Mickey Burke and Graham Reilly.

A game that will live with each person forever.

Author: Fergal Lynch
Hardback: €25.00
Paperback: €20.00
Ebook: €9.99
ISBN: 9781910827338

Buy on **Amazon**
(and paperback available in all good bookstores)

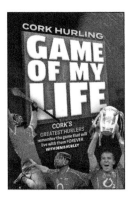

CORK LGFA

GAME OF MY LIFE

25 OF THE GREATEST CORK ladies footballers over the last 60 years remember the one game in their careers that defined their sporting lives.

Including: Juliet Murphy, Mary O'Connor, Rena Buckley, Elaine Harte, Nollaig Cleary, Bríd Stack, Norita Kelly, Geraldine O'Flynn, Martina O'Brien, Marie Ambrose, Valerie Mupcahy, Angela Walsh, Deirdre O'Reilly, Briege Corkery, Ciara O'Sullivan, Áine Terry O'Sullivan, Shauna Kelly, Orlagh Farmer, Emma Spillane, Eimear Scally, Orla Finn, Saoirse Noonan, Doireann O'Sullivan, Hannah Looney, Melissa Duggan.

A game that will live with each person forever.

Author: Ger McCarthy
Hardback: €25.00
Paperback: €20.00
Ebook: €9.99
ISBN: 9781910827499

Buy on **Amazon**
(and paperback available in all good bookstores)

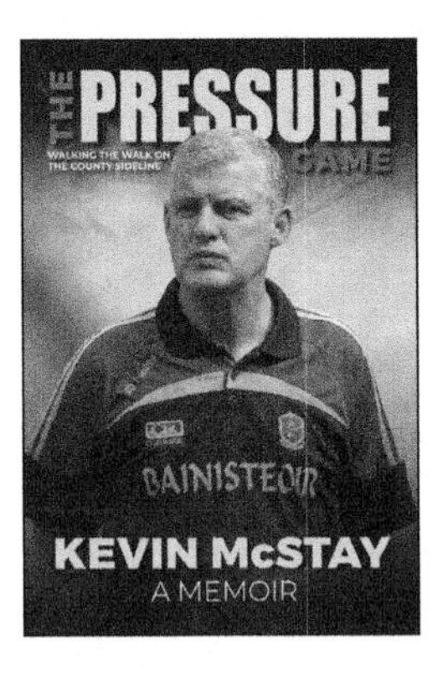

The Pressure Game

Kevin McStay: An Autobiography

FOR THE FIRST time one of the top GAA managers in the country has revealed the inside story of what it's like to 'Walk the Walk on a County Sideline'. Former Mayo Allstar footballer Kevin McStay gave up 20 years of working as a commentator and analyst on RTE's Sunday Game to take up the position of Roscommon team manager in 2016.

The whole country watched to see how he would survive on the sideline – and how he would face up to the pressures of facing Jim's Gavin's Dublin, Mayo and Kerry and Tyrone, on the toughest stage in Gaelic football.

In his three years in charge, McStay led Roscommon to a Connacht title in 2017 and a prized place in the Super 8s in 2018 before quitting the job. He has now returned to the RTE broadcasting booth.

This is the amazing inside story of the ***The Pressure Game***.

Authors: Kevin McStay with Liam Hayes

Hardback: €25.00

Paperback: €20.00

Ebook: €9.99

ISBN: 9781910827086

Buy on **Amazon**

(and paperback available in all good bookstores)

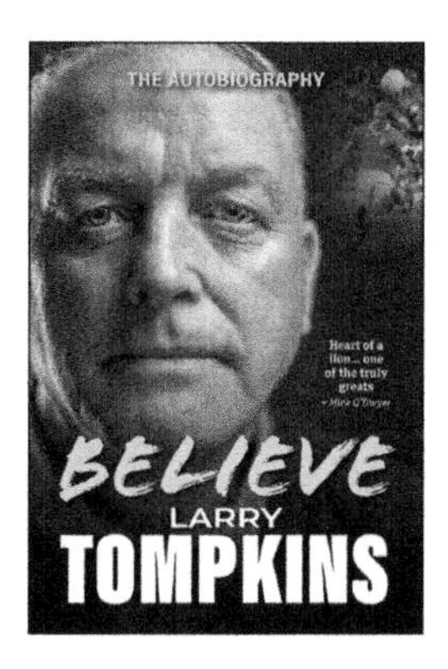

BELIEVE

Larry Tompkins: An Autobiography

HIS SELF-BELIEF WAS unbreakable. His iron will inspirational. Nothing could stop Larry Tompkins. No man, no team, as he made his football life the greatest story ever told in the long and brilliant history of the GAA.

Six years with his native Kildare left him empty-handed and heartbroken. He emigrated to New York to find a job and find a team he could lead to championship glory. In the United States, Tompkins' belief in himself never dimmed. He led Donegal to four New York championships in the Big Apple. He also found a new home for himself in Ireland and led Castlehaven to two Cork and Munster titles. In between, he also became the most valuable and feared footballer in Ireland.

BELIEVE is the story of a man who defied all the odds. In Cork's magnificent red shirt, he led his adopted county to two All-Ireland titles in 1989 and 90, one National League and six Munster titles, and he also was honoured with three All Star awards. Upon his retirement, Larry Tompkins continued to lead and inspire, and make others believe too.

Authors: Larry Tompkins with Denis Hurley

Hardback: €25.00

Paperback: €20.00

Ebook: €9.99

ISBN: 9781910827123

Buy on **Amazon**

(and paperback available in all good bookstores)

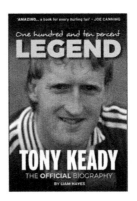

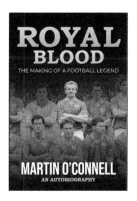

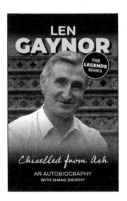

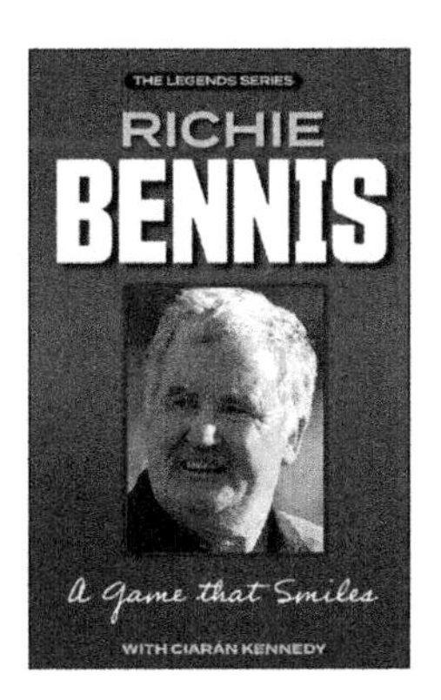

'A Game that Smiles'

The Richie Bennis Autobiography

RICHIE BENNIS IS one of the true legends remaining in the game of hurling. A towering figure in Limerick GAA, he played a central role as the county won the All-Ireland title in 1973 and then he strived as hard as anyone to see the Liam MacCarthy Cup return to the Treaty County.

It was a wait of 45 years – during which time Bennis worked at grassroots hurling in the famed Patrickswell club, where he hurled into his 40s and won 10 county titles. He also led Limerick as team manager to the 2007 All-Ireland final where they lost to Kilkenny.

In 2018, Limerick were crowned All-Ireland champions.

For Richie Bennis, a long agonising wait ended. His story is one of triumph, and heartache and personal tragedy, and a courage that was never dimmed.

Authors: Richie Bennis with Ciarán Kennedy

Hardback: €25.00

Paperback: €20.00

Ebook: €9.99

ISBN: 9781910827093

Buy on **Amazon**

(and paperback available in all good bookstores)

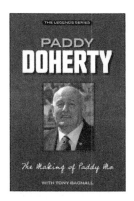

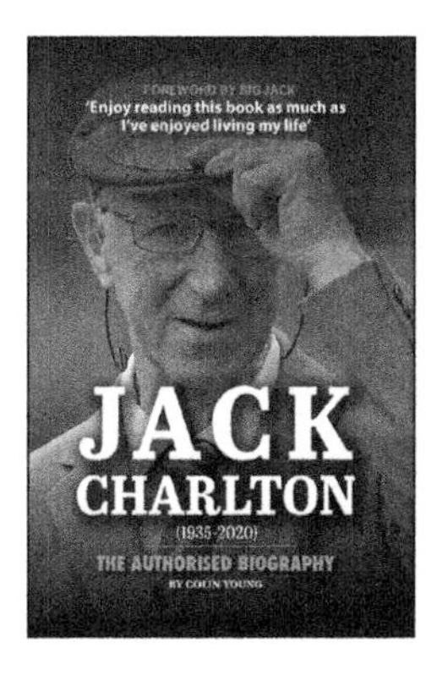

Jack Charlton

The Authorised Biography

AS ONE OF the true legends of Irish and English football, Jack Charlton was a man both loved and feared, but now the people who have lived with him all of his life introduce the real 'Big Jack' in this brilliant authorised biography which is presented in a foreword by Jack himself.

For the first time Jack's wife and family, his teammates as a World Cup winner with England in 1966, and his players during his management years with Middlesbrough, Sheffield Wednesday, Newcastle, and Ireland tell their stories of the man who dominated their lives. Graeme Souness, Chris Waddle, and Peter Beardsley amongst others, are joined by Mick McCarthy, Niall Quinn and the greatest footballers who played under Big Jack for 10 years as Ireland team boss.

This is the most personable, inviting and intimate account of Jack Charlton's life, and the book contains photographs published for the first time from Jack and Pat Charlton's personal collection.

Author: Colin Young

Hardback: €25.00

Paperback: €20.00

Ebook: €9.99

ISBN: 9781910827017

Buy on **Amazon**

(and paperback available in all good bookstores)

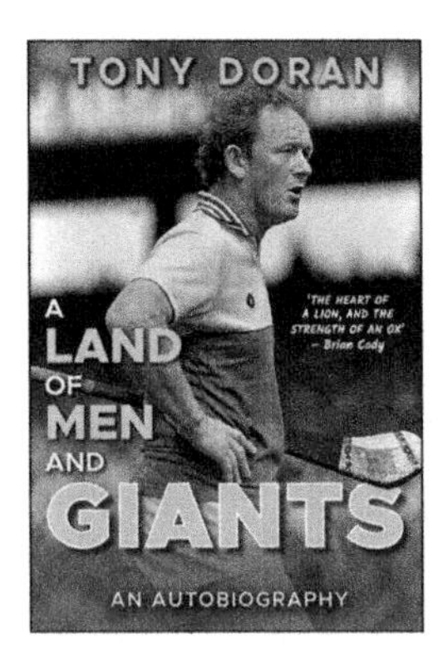

A Land of Men and Giants

The Tony Doran Autobiography

WEXFORD'S ALL-IRELAND winning hero Tony Doran was a giant in the game of hurling through the 1960s, 70s and 80s, at a time when full-forwards were ordered to plunder goals. In his 19 years and 187 appearances as a Wexford hurler, Tony Doran successfully went for goal 131 times. But Doran also played against giants from Kilkenny, Tipperary and Cork, and so many other counties, at a time when the game of hurling tested the wits and the courage of every man on the field.

Some of these men became giants.

A Land of Men and Giants is the story told by Tony Doran of a life spent living and competing against legendary men and true giants of the game.

A Land of Men and Giants: The Autobiography of Tony Doran is edited by award-winning writer and author Liam Hayes.

Authors: Tony Doran with Liam Hayes

Hardback: €25.00

Paperback: €20.00

Ebook: €9.99

ISBN: 9781910827031

Buy on **Amazon**

(and paperback available in all good bookstores)

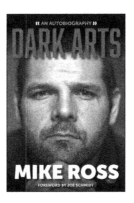

Printed in Great Britain
by Amazon